At ✳ Iss

Islam in America

Laura K. Egendorf, *Book Editor*

Bruce Glassman, *Vice President*
Bonnie Szumski, *Publisher*
Helen Cothran, *Managing Editor*

GREENHAVEN PRESS
An imprint of Thomson Gale, a part of The Thomson Corporation

THOMSON

GALE

Detroit • New York • San Francisco • San Diego • New Haven, Conn.
Waterville, Maine • London • Munich

LIBRARY OF CONGRESS CATALOGING-IN-PUBLICATION DATA

Islam in America / Laura K. Egendorf, book editor.
 p. cm. — (At issue)
Includes bibliographical references and index.
ISBN 0-7377-2727-6 (lib. : alk. paper) — ISBN 0-7377-2728-4 (pbk. : alk. paper)
 1. Islam—United States. 2. Muslims—United States. I. Egendorf, Laura K.,
1973– . II. At issue (San Diego, Calif.)
BP67.U6I87 2006
297'.0973—dc22

2005046317

Printed in the United States of America

Contents

Introduction

"If the Muslim community continues to grow at the present rate, by the year 2015 Islam will be the second largest religion in the United States."
—Yvonne Haddad, professor of history, Georgetown University

Although Islam has been practiced in the United States since the seventeenth century, most Americans were largely unfamiliar with the religion until the terrorist attacks of September 11, 2001. The attacks were perpetrated by self-proclaimed Muslim fanatics, who had come to the United States from the Middle East, primarily Saudi Arabia. They hijacked four commercial airliners and flew two of them into the World Trade Center in New York City and the other into the Pentagon in Washington, D.C. The fourth plane crashed in a field in Pennsylvania. Over three thousand people died in the attacks. That cataclysmic event prompted both a greater interest in and a greater fear of Islam. While American Muslims make up only a small percentage of the U.S. population (estimates range between 2 and 9 million), they are a diverse group with growing influence—an influence that some Americans have expressed concern about, arguing that radical forms of Islam are establishing a foothold in the United States.

Regardless of the particular version of Islam practiced, its more than one billion adherents follow five precepts: worshipping one deity, whose messenger is Muhammad; praying five times each day; giving charity to the poor and needy; fasting during the daylight hours of Ramadan, health permitting; and making at least one ritual pilgrimage to Mecca, if such a trip can be afforded.

While Islam may be easier to follow for Muslims living in nations where it is the majority religion, it nevertheless has a strong foothold in the United States. Although the number of American Muslims remains fairly small, the population is growing, and within a decade, Muslims may well outnumber American Catholics. The faith reached American shores via the slave trade—even now, African Americans make up the majority of Muslim Americans, representing 42 percent of the population. The first Muslims to arrive in the United States of their own free will were from the Middle East. About 12.4 percent of American Muslims today come from Middle Eastern nations. Immigrants from Southeast Asia comprise 24 percent of Muslims in America, and the remaining number consists of European Muslims, and Latino and white converts.

As the Muslim population increases in the United States, so do questions about whether American Muslims are turning toward moderate interpretations of the faith, which decry violence and terrorism, or whether they are becoming adherents to the more radical and violent sects. Some commentators argue that American mosques and Islamic schools are breeding grounds for violent and anti-American sentiments. In its report *Saudi Publications on Hate Ideology Invade American Mosques*, the Center for Religious Freedom asserts that the particularly radical Wahhabi sect has, with the financial assistance of the Saudi Arabian government, been able to inundate American Muslim institutions with extremist texts. According to the center, "The message of these Saudi government Wahhabi publications and authoritative religious rulings is designed to breed greater aloofness, instill suspicion, and ultimately engender hatred for America and its people." Journalist and author Stephen Schwartz contends in his June 2003 article, "Reading, Writing, and Extremism," published in the *Weekly Standard*, that Islamic academies throughout the United States, many of which are funded by the Saudi government, propagate views "just as conducive to political extremism and even terrorism as those taught in the extremist madrasas [religious schools] of Pakistan or Saudi Arabia itself." Schwartz observes that these academies use books published in Saudi Arabia that urge jihad—or holy war—against non-Muslims.

On the other hand, many American Muslims repudiate radicalism and deny that it has a strong influence on their faith—an assertion made long before the September 11 attacks. In a June 2000 interview with *Middle East Quarterly*, Muhammad Hisham Kabbani, the chairman of the Islamic Supreme Council of America, declares, "We Muslims should speak about Islamic moderation, about the Islamic way to a better life. . . . We have a responsibility not to impose an ideological agenda on the political scene." Notably, American Muslims spoke out forcefully against the September 11 attacks. Karima Diane Alavi, the founding director of Islamic World Educational Services, wrote in the magazine *America* in March 2002, "We American Muslims [are] still reeling from the fact that our faith had also been hijacked on Sept. 11 by people who twisted their version of Islam into a blackened form." President George W. Bush put his weight behind this claim when he said, "These acts of violence against innocents violate the fundamental tenets of the Islamic faith, and it's important for my fellow Americans to understand that. . . . The face of terror is not the true faith of Islam. That's not what Islam is all about. Islam is peace."

The growing presence of Muslims in America, combined with the September 11 attacks, has raised many questions about the role Islam will play in America's future. In *At Issue: Islam in America*, the authors debate the many ways that the religion has influenced life in the United States and explore how American Muslims have been treated since the terrorist attacks of September 11, 2001.

1

Islam Is a Positive Force in America

Zaheer Uddin

Zaheer Uddin is the executive director of the Center for American Muslim Research and Information.

Islam has a long history in the United States. While the first two waves of Muslims came from Africa, often on slave ships, followers of Islam later came from the Middle East, Asia, and southern Europe. In addition, many Americans have converted to Islam. Although some Americans blamed Islam for the September 11, 2001, terrorist attacks, American Muslims condemned the attacks. Islam is a peaceful religion, and its followers are well-educated, successful people who contribute positively to America.

Islam is the fastest growing religion in the world, especially in the United States. From Indonesia to Morocco, there are 56 countries where Muslims are a majority and several dozen more where they are a sizable minority.

Every fourth person on this planet is a Muslim. Muslims come from all races and countries. Islamic civilization has made tremendous achievements in science and produced some of the most prominent scientists in previous centuries. Al-Khwarizmi introduced Arabic numerals to the West in the ninth century; Rhazes (ar-Razi) described and treated smallpox in the tenth century; Avicenna (Ibn Sina) diagnosed and treated meningitis in the eleventh century; Al-Shirazi explained the cause of rainbows in the thirteenth century; and Ibn Kashani invented a computing machine in the fifteenth century. But Islam is still a misunderstood religion in the West.

A Brief History of Islam in America

The advent of Islam to America can be divided into four periods:

First era. There are some claims that Muslims came to America before Columbus. A number of linguists, historians, and archaeologists have postulated that Arabic-speaking Muslims from North Africa came to the Americas in the seventh century. Islamic coins have been found in America dating from the ninth to eleventh centuries; Muslim names and other Islamic words are engraved on Nevada bedrock in ancient Kufic Arabic dating from sometime after 650. Such Muslims could have come as traders and gone back home to the Kingdom of Mali in northwest Africa.

Second era. For 400 years, hundreds of thousands of African slaves were brought to the New World. According to reliable estimates, some 7 to 30 percent of them were Muslims. Despite their forced separation from Muslim lands and culture, scores of documented reports hold that Muslim slaves maintained some form of their faith. One of the most famous was Kunta Kinte, hero of the best-seller by Alex Haley and the popular TV series *Roots*.

> *The history of Islam in America is not just the story of immigrant Muslims but of conversions of indigenous people.*

Third era. Between the mid-nineteenth century and the early twentieth century, thousands of Muslims came to America from the area of Shaam (present-day Syria, Jordan, and Lebanon), Palestine, British India, southern Europe (Bosnia, Yugoslavia, and Albania), Turkey, central Asia, and Ukraine. These Muslims were primarily poor. Most of them were understandably more concerned with finding a living in America than with keeping their Islamic culture. However, they built a few mosques or rented homes for community prayers.

Cedar Rapids, Iowa, has the oldest continuously existing Muslim community in America today. Three brothers (Musa,

Ali, and Abbas) found their way there in 1885. By 1912, some 35 young Muslims from Syria and Lebanon had joined them. In 1920, they established a temporary mosque and laid the foundation for what would be the first mosque in the Midwest. The project was completed in 1934.

Amanat Ali Khan, who came to Sacramento in 1912, was the first immigrant from what is now Pakistan. Shortly thereafter, many Pakistanis progressed from being farm laborers to farm owners in the Sacramento area. Pakistani farmers also played a major role in developing agriculture in the Imperial Valley of Arizona.

> *American Muslims are prominent in engineering, medicine, business, education, and sports.*

During this period, mosques were founded in Connecticut, Michigan, and Brooklyn. The Young Men's Muslim Association was founded in 1923. Many Muslim communities became totally assimilated into the larger melting pot; their distinct Islamic identity gradually vanished.

Fourth era. After World War II, particularly in the late 1960s, U.S. immigration law allowed people from all countries to migrate to the United States on a merit basis. Since then, great numbers of Muslim students and professionals, mainly medical doctors and engineers, have come to America for education and employment. These new immigrants, with the financial support of international Islamic organizations and some Muslim governments, established mosques and Islamic centers as well as national and professional Islamic organizations. One of the largest, the Islamic Center in Washington, D.C., was inaugurated by President Eisenhower in 1957.

Indigenous Movements

The history of Islam in America is not just the story of immigrant Muslims but of conversions of indigenous people. It is a misconception that African Americans were the first to accept Islam. On the contrary, the first recorded American convert to Islam was a European American, the Reverend Norman, a

Methodist missionary who went to Turkey and became a Muslim in the 1870s. Another prominent convert was Alexander Russell Webb, a journalist and son of a newspaper editor and publisher. In 1887, as U.S. consul general in the Philippines, he corresponded with Badaruddin Abdullah Kur, a prominent Indian Muslim official in Bombay. In the process he converted to Islam in 1891. He resigned his diplomatic service, toured India, and met Muslim leaders and scholars for two months. After returning to New York in early 1893, he founded an organization called the American Islamic Propaganda Movement.

Before Webb's death, Islam emerged as a religious and nationalistic phenomenon among African Americans. Early major Muslim communities established by African Americans include the Moorish Science Temple (1913), the Universal Islamic Society (1926), the Islamic Brotherhood (1928), the Nation of Islam (1930), and the Islamic Mission Society (1939).

Some well-known Muslim personalities came on the horizon through these indigenous Islamic movements. Most notable are Muhammad Ali, Malcolm X, and Kareem Abdul Jabbar.

The Demographics of Muslim Americans

Muslims live almost everywhere in the United States, having become part of the great mosaic. The present-day Muslim community consists of almost all races, nationalities, and ethnicities. Muslims are well-educated, law-abiding, and successful professionals. The majority of Muslims live in big cities and their suburbs, including New York City, Chicago, Houston, Los Angeles, the San Francisco Bay area, and Dallas.

There are no government census figures about the number of Muslims in America. Some organizations have done their own surveys and have come up with different numbers, varying from 1.5 to 10 million. The most reliable study on this subject, done by the Center for American Muslim Research and Information (CAMRI) in 1998, found that seven million Muslims live in the United States. (This figure will probably double by 2022.) The Muslim population is also very young. Nearly half are 20 or younger, while 50.5 percent fall between 20 and 65. Only 0.5 percent can be called aged. Muslim males outnumber females by only 4 percentage points: there are 104 males for every 100 females on an average.

U.S. Muslims represent all 185-plus countries that are in the United Nations. A large chunk of them represent three distinct ethnicities: Arab (first and second generation), 32.7 percent; indigenous American (African American and European American), 29.5 percent; and South Asians (Pakistani, Indian, and Bangladeshi), 29.3 percent.

Muslims are highly educated. The average working Muslim, according to the CAMRI report, has three years of college education (two years beyond the American average). Likewise, as a whole, Muslims are between middle- and upper-middle-income brackets. According to the report, their median yearly income averages $39,700 (as of 1997). The largest number (49.4 percent) are in engineering and computer sciences, 11.6 percent are in medicine and related professions, and 10.5 percent are in business administration and finance.

> *Many find in Islam a solace for their spiritual and social needs.*

Muslims have established religious, educational, and charity institutions. There are over 1,600 mosques in the United States, and more than 160 full-time Islamic schools. Over 200,000 Muslim businesses range from corner stores to big corporations. Muslims run three universities, including the world's first live Internet-based Islamic university.

American Muslims are prominent in engineering, medicine, business, education, and sports. Muslim chief executive officers of major industries include Farooq Kathwari of Ethan Allen Furniture, Ray Irani of Occidental Petroleum, and Safi Qureshi of AST Computers. Muslims are also in the news media and entertainment. Most prominent are Mustafa Akkad and Assad Kelada, producers of motion pictures and television series, and Fareed Zakaria, editor of *Newsweek International.* Distinguished professors and medical doctors work in almost every major university and hospital. In 1999, Ahmed Zewail, a professor at the California Institute of Technology, received the Nobel Prize in chemistry.

The Tenets of Islam

Muslims are followers of Islam, which, in Arabic, means *submission* and *peace.* Islam is an Abrahamic faith, springing from the monotheism of the great patriarch of Christianity, Judaism, and Islam. Islamic life is based on a solid foundation of belief and action. Both must go together.

The teachings of Islam are based on the oneness and uniqueness of God (Allah) and the accountability of man. After death, reward and punishment are distributed according to a person's deeds in this life. For the guidance of humanity, Allah selected prophets and messengers. Muslims believe that Adam, Noah, Abraham, Moses, and Jesus were prophets. This chain concluded with the Prophet Muhammad. Therefore, a Muslim's faith cannot be complete unless he believes in Moses and Jesus.

Allah also has revealed scriptures to Abraham, Moses, Jesus, and Muhammad. The Qur'an, revealed to Muhammad, is the direct word of Allah in pure form. It is to be followed for all time.

The Prophet Muhammad is loved and revered by Muslims because he was chosen by Allah and because he practiced the teachings of Islam in his own life. Therefore, he is the role model for Muslims everywhere. He is not considered to be divine but a perfect human being. He was born in 570 and passed away in 633 in Arabia.

A person who accepts Islamic beliefs is expected to follow them in his actions. Therefore, after declaring that there is none worthy of worship except Allah and Muhammad is His messenger, he has to perform five daily prayers, fast in the month of Ramadan, pay tithes, and make a pilgrimage to Mecca.

Men and women are equal in Islam in terms of responsibilities, rights, and duties. Islam places a strong emphasis on family values, dignity, justice, and fair play in the social, economical, and political life of individuals or societies.

The majority of Muslims believe that the followers of the three great religions, Christianity, Judaism, and Islam, have much in common in principles and practices. They also believe in the need to develop more understanding and cooperation to solve today's problems, so that all people can achieve real peace and justice.

American Muslims After September 11

American Muslims were overcome with grief after the [September 11, 2001, terrorist attacks] and they mourned the deaths of their countrymen. But they experienced something else: a lingering sadness for Islam, a faith they felt had been grossly abused. They condemned the attack in unequivocal terms, arranged blood drives, and donated generously as they deeply felt the pain of those who were touched by the tragedy. Unfortunately, some mosques and Islamic centers were targeted for arson, and many Muslims experienced personal hostility in their own neighborhoods. Over one thousand Muslims and Arab Christians were detained based on mere suspicion.

But American Muslims see a silver lining. Many Americans are now trying to learn about Islam and Muslims as they contemplate the deeds of religious extremists. "Americans have bought more flags since September 11, but they've also bought more Qur'ans," says Imam Siraj Wahhaj. "I've had more converts since September 11, and I've spoken in so many different forums and interfaith meetings."

Many find in Islam a solace for their spiritual and social needs; they are intrigued by its ideas and humane approach to world problems. Muslims hope that once the hateful gazes and vengeful acts subside, they will be able to resume their normal life in the land of the free and hopeful.

2

Radical Islam Is a Harmful Force in America

Stephen Schwartz

Stephen Schwartz, a journalist who writes regularly on Islam and terrorism, is the author of The Two Faces of Islam: Saudi Fundamentalism and Its Role in Terrorism.

The extremist form of Islam known as Wahhabism is gaining power in the United States. The Wahhabi establishment in America is backed by Saudi Arabia—where Wahhabism is widely practiced. It controls most American mosques and prominent Muslim organizations. In addition, virtually all Islamic chaplains in the U.S. prison and military systems are Wahhabis, and Islamic schools throughout the United States are supported by Saudi money and teach Wahhabi principles. Wahhabi ideology, which is anti-American and antidemocratic, is spreading throughout the American Muslim community. The U.S. government and media must take steps to reduce the spread of Muslim extremism by investigating the extent of Wahhabi influence and by publicizing the works of moderate Muslims in America and throughout the world.

When the horror of [the terrorist attacks of September 11, 2001] happened, Americans experienced a great deal of confusion and heard a great deal of speculation about the motives for anti-American terrorism. It was natural for most of us to assume that we were attacked because of who we are: because we are wealthy, because we are a dominant power in the world and because we represent ideas that are in conflict with the ideas of radical Islam. Many also assumed—wrongly I think—that it had mostly to do with the Middle East and Israel. But almost immediately a very interesting fact emerged: of the 19 suicide terrorists on September 11, 15 were subjects of the kingdom of Saudi Arabia.

> *The Saudis decided to create an American Islamic establishment based on the radical doctrines of Wahhabism.*

Why is this important? It is important because these were not poor people from refugee camps on the West Bank or in Gaza. These were not people who had grown up feeling some grievance against Israel and the United States because they lived in difficult conditions. These were not people from the crowded and disrupted communities of Egypt or Pakistan, or people who had experienced anti-Islamic violence in the last 20 years and had therefore turned against the United States. These people had grown up in the country that Americans often think of as our most solid and dependable ally in the Arab world—the kingdom of Saudi Arabia. Thus the question arose: Why would Saudis be involved in this?

Related questions followed: What does it mean that [terrorist leader] Osama Bin Laden is a Saudi? And that so many members of Al-Qaeda [terrorist group] are Saudis? Why is it that Al-Qaeda is essentially a Saudi political movement? And that 25 percent of those detained in Guantanamo [Bay, Cuba, detention center for terrorists] are Saudis? Why is it that a country the U.S. had favored, to which the U.S. had delivered an enormous amount of wealth through the purchase of oil—a country that the U.S. had protected militarily, and whose young people have been educated in America for many years—why was Saudi Arabia, of all countries, so connected to the attacks of September 11?

Osama Bin Laden's Message

Many in the United States bought into Osama Bin Laden's propaganda when he claimed to be outraged that American troops were stationed on the "holy soil" of Saudi Arabia. In fact, American troops were *never* stationed on Saudi "holy soil," because Riyadh, the capital of Saudi Arabia, and Dhahran, the area where most U.S. troops were stationed, are not Islamic holy sites. The only holy places in Saudi Arabia, from the Muslim perspective, are Mecca and Medina—and there were never American troops in either of those cities. The only time foreign troops were sent to Mecca or Medina was in 1979, when a group of Muslim radicals took over the Grand Mosque in Mecca and the Saudi government sent in French paratroops to kill them.

We are accustomed to hearing that Osama Bin Laden and Al-Qaeda look on the Saudi royal family as just as much an enemy as the U.S., and that they want to overthrow it. But the truth, as I first pointed out in the *Weekly Standard* about a month after September 11, is that Osama Bin Laden has *never* called for the overthrow of the Saudi royal family. What he calls for is a change in their policies. That is, he calls for what he would consider a more Islamic policy. The fact is—based on my contacts and interviews with Saudi subjects both inside and outside the kingdom—Osama is essentially a *product* of the Saudi regime, and in particular of the hardliners in the regime. And so the message of Osama Bin Laden on September 11 was also a message from those Saudi hardliners, and the message was aimed at their audiences.

> *Every single Islamic chaplain in the U.S. military has been certified by Saudi-controlled groups.*

First, it was a message to the United States saying, "Don't ask Saudi Arabia to change, because if we change, this is what you'll get—instead of us, Osama."

Second, it was a message to the people of Saudi Arabia—a fundamentally rational people. Many Saudis are on the Internet. Many have satellite dishes. And they are surrounded by a crescent of normalizing countries: Iraq, Kuwait, Qatar, Bahrain, the Emirates, Oman, Yemen—countries that certainly are not as progressive and prosperous as Florida, but that are on their way toward becoming normal modern countries. And yet Saudis live in a country—to cite but one of several examples of stifling backwardness—where women are not allowed to drive. So Saudi society is a society demanding change. And the second message of September 11 was to the Saudi people in response to their yearning: "Don't try to make changes because we radical Islamists still have enormous power, and it is a destructive power."

Third, the same message was intended for Muslims all around the world: "Don't challenge our control over global Islam."

The Rise of Wahhabism in the United States

The ideology of Saudi hardliners is, unfortunately, of great relevance even inside the United States. One doctrine of Islam dominates in Saudi Arabia: It is called Wahhabism. Wahhabism is the most extreme, the most violent, the most separatist, the most expansionistic form of Islam that exists. It's a form of Islam that not only lashes out at the West, but that seeks to take over and impose a rigid conformity on the whole Muslim world.

What then of America? Islam was new in the United States in the 1980s and 1990s. Then, because of changes in the immigration laws, the American Muslim community suddenly became much larger. Most Muslims who came to the United States were not Arabs. The plurality have been people from Pakistan, India and Bangladesh. And as Islam originally emerged as a major religion in the U.S., it—unlike other American religions —didn't have an establishment. A disparate group of Muslims arrived and established mosques in various places. They represented different ethnic groups and lacked any structure to bring them together and unite them. But that didn't last long. And why? Because the Saudis decided to create an American Islamic establishment based on the radical doctrines of Wahhabism. In order to bring this about, they created a system of organizations that would speak for American Muslims to the government and the media and through the educational system and the mosques.

One can learn a lot about how the Saudi-backed Wahhabi establishment in the U.S. works by looking at how it came to speak for all of Islam in the American media. It did this by creating a set of organizations. One of the most prominent is called the Council on American-Islamic Relations (CAIR). This group was allegedly set up to be a kind of a Muslim version of the Jewish Anti-Defamation League. That is, its stated goal was to protect Muslims against prejudice and stereotypes. I was working in the newsroom of the *San Francisco Chronicle* at the time, and I was struck by CAIR's approach with our reporters and editors. They didn't come to the newspaper offices and say, "Were Muslims; were here now; this is our holy book; this is the life of our prophet Muhammad; these are the holidays we observe; this is what we believe in, and we'd like you to report these things accurately." Rather, they came and they said, "We are a minority and we suffer from discrimination. We suffer from hurtful stereotypes. We know that you are good liberal reporters, and that you want to avoid inflicting these stereotypes on us. So whenever you do a story on Islam, you should call us first and make sure it is correct." And, of course, that meant "correct" according to Saudi-sponsored Wahhabism.

There are other such groups. One of them is called the Islamic Society of North America. It is directly controlled from Saudi Arabia, and openly owns 250 of the 1,200 main mosques in the United States. But this is just the tip of the iceberg: My research suggests that a full 80 percent of American mosques are under the control of the Saudi government and Wahhabism. This does not mean that 80 percent of American Muslims are supporters of Wahhabism—only that their mosques are controlled by the Saudi Wahhabis. There's a range of such organizations. Many we don't hear much about, including some of the worst; for example, the Islamic Circle of North America, which acts as a kind of extremist militia among Pakistani Muslims and has a very bad reputation for threatening, intimidating and enforcing conformity in the Pakistani Muslim community.

Wahhabism in Prisons, the Military, and Schools

There are three other areas where the Saudi government and its Wahhabi ideology have gained tremendous influence in the U.S. The first is in the American prison system. With one single exception, all of the federal and state chaplains representing Islam in American prisons are Wahhabis. That is, they are certified by groups originating in Saudi Arabia; the curriculum they follow was created in Saudi Arabia; and they go into our prisons and preach an extremist doctrine. This is not the same as saying that they go into our prisons and directly recruit terrorists—although there *have* been cases of that. But anytime you go into a prison—an environment of violence, obviously populated by troubled people—and preach an extremist doctrine, there are going to be bad and dangerous consequences.

The second area is in the military services. Every single Islamic chaplain in the U.S. military has been certified by Saudi-controlled groups—which means that our military chaplains also hold to Wahhabi doctrines. Is it surprising, then, that we had the incident of the Muslim solider in Kuwait who attacked his fellow soldiers? Or the problems with military personnel at Guantanamo? Or the Muslim military man in Washington State who was trying to turn over useful information to Al-Qaeda?

And finally there is the problem with what are known as the Islamic academies: Islamic elementary schools, middle schools and high schools throughout the U.S. that are supported by Saudi money and preach the Saudi-Wahhabi doctrine—in some cases to Saudi expatriate children living here, but in many other cases to Muslim children who are U.S. citizens.

Stemming Extremism

This seems a very dark picture. On the other hand, there are some fairly simple steps to take to solve the problem.

First and foremost, it is important to support the federal and state governments in a sustained investigation of Islamic extremism in our country. That means not falling for the propaganda claim—made by groups like CAIR—that investigating what's happening in mosques, and the literature being distributed in mosques, somehow violates religious freedom. It is not a violation of religious freedom to prevent extremists from using religion as a cover for sedition and criminality. To the contrary, preventing this is necessary to the defense of religious freedom. So it's absolutely necessary to support the FBI, the Justice Department, and other agencies who are investigating the extent to which Islam in the United States is under the influence of anti-American, anti-democratic extremists. And it is important that they are empowered to perform these investigations with laws like the Patriot Act.

Second, we must identify and support the moderate and patriotic Muslims in the United States who oppose Wahhabism and all it stands for. Many Muslims fit this description, even if we rarely hear of them.

Related to this, we should hold the media to account for its coverage of these issues. How many times have we heard the question since September 11: "Why is it that more Muslim leaders didn't speak out against this abomination?" Actually, many Muslim leaders did speak out against terrorism and in support of freedom, but they weren't heard in the media because their message didn't fit the mold that the media likes to impose on this story. Thus, for instance, we didn't hear from a Muslim leader in Chicago—the Mufti of the Bosnian Muslims in America—who is a very influential man, who loves America, and who, the day after September 11, said, "No Muslim living in America should support any of this. Everybody should do everything possible to stop it. If you hear about it in your community, tell the FBI about it and organize against it." Instead, what the media covered were angry Muslims blaming America's support of Israel and other misleading factors.

I say to my fellow journalists, "Why don't you go to countries like Malaysia, Indonesia, Bangladesh, West Africa, Morocco and Bosnia? Why don't you go and interview the Muslim leaders who support the West, who are against terrorism and who are willing to stand alongside the United States?" Recently (as I have written in the *Weekly Standard*), I went to Uzbekistan and interviewed three Islamist defectors, two of them from Al-Qaeda. These interviews suggest that although the leaders of the Islamist movement are extreme, murderous and fanatical, the foot soldiers in the movement are just like foot soldiers in other extremist movements. They get involved in this movement for reasons that are not ideological, and often become disillusioned. One man I spoke to defected from a group connected to Al-Qaeda when he saw that he was being used to commit atrocities against his own comrades. At the end of the interview, I asked him if he had anything to say to Americans. "Yes," he said, "I want you to tell President [George W.] Bush there are a lot of us out here who are ready to stand alongside America to deal a death blow to these monsters, these terrorists."

As this story indicates, there is reason to be optimistic about the war on terror around the globe. But let us also not forget, in the course of conducting that war, the importance of employing law enforcement to stem the influence of Saudi-supported Wahhabi extremism in our own country.

3

Some American Muslim Organizations Support Terrorist Groups

J. Michael Waller

J. Michael Waller is a senior writer for Insight on the News.

Some American Muslim organizations, most notably the American Muslim Council (AMC), are undermining the U.S. war on terrorism by supporting terrorists and lobbying to weaken antiterrorism measures. The AMC has a long history of promoting terrorist causes, with its officials publicly proclaiming allegiance to terrorist organizations such as Hezbollah and refusing to condemn their deadly activities. In addition, the council and its allied groups have discouraged American Muslims from assisting law-enforcement officers in antiterrorism cases and have sought to influence the White House and Congress in an effort to abolish or prevent the passage of antiterrorism measures such as the USA PATRIOT Act.

Terrorists and their supporters are doing their best to weave themselves into the political fabric of American society, say specialists in homeland security. They are operating front groups and charities to finance their operations, and they are running influence operations to weaken federal antiterrorism laws under the guise of protecting civil liberties.

The Feb. 20 [2003] arrest of an alleged leader of the Palestinian Islamic Jihad (PIJ), operating what the FBI calls a Tampa-based terrorist cell under cover as a professor at the University of South Florida (USF), has exposed one suspected operation. In doing so it has turned media focus on political groups that had been working in Washington with the accused, Sami Al-Arian, and set White House officials pointing fingers at one another about how the alleged terrorist managed to be included in the administration's controversial Muslim-outreach program.

That outreach effort, with its roots in the George W. Bush 2000 presidential campaign, has provoked controversy among the United States' growing Muslim and Arab-American communities, as well as among security-minded supporters of the president. Critics allege favoritism toward a small but vocal cadre of groups they say support terrorism. Mainstream Muslim and Arab-American organizations that were shut out of the liaison effort tell *Insight* that extremists spent large sums trying to buy access in an effort to hijack the Bush administration's initiative, obtaining repeated meetings at the White House and with the president himself to acquire political cover and claim legitimacy.

Weakening Antiterrorism Laws

The FBI's arrest of USF professor Al-Arian illustrates the problem. According to federal law-enforcement sources, Al-Arian was a principal organizer, trainer and coach for lobbying campaigns designed to eviscerate federal antiterrorism laws that had a particularly damaging effect on terrorist-support activities inside the United States. He was, say the sources, an architect of a years-long effort to repeal federal laws permitting prosecutors to use highly classified information in the arrest and detention of foreigners suspected of terrorist ties, without permitting the suspects to know the evidence. The law is intended for terrorist cases where the suspect's knowledge of extremely sensitive evidence could, among other things, result in the murders of Muslims and others who helped law-enforcement officials identify and build cases against terrorist operations.

Decrying the "secret-evidence" laws as unfairly "targeting" all Muslims and ethnic Arabs, Al-Arian portrayed their abolition as a civil-rights issue, appealing to liberal civil-liberties groups, libertarians and small-government conservatives to join forces against Big Brother. The same groups, an *Insight* investigation shows, worked after the Sept. 11, 2001, al-Qaeda airliner attacks to gut the Bush administration's tough new antiterrorism package—the very laws the FBI eventually would use to take down Al-Arian, whom it had been watching for years, and the PIJ's network inside the United States.

Count No. 42 of the 50-count federal grand-jury indictment of Al-Arian and other defendants alleged that the PIJ "would and did seek to obtain support from influential individuals in the United States under the guise of promoting and protecting Arab rights." Al-Arian worked with several Washington-based groups, including the American Muslim Council (AMC) and the Islamic Institute, as part of his alleged influence operations. He was the first speaker at the lobbyist-training seminars at the AMC's 2000 and 2001 national conventions. He coached council members and others on lobbying Congress to influence legislation and statutes designed to give federal authorities the legal tools necessary to build cases against his and other alleged terrorist-support activities and to use that evidence in a court of law to try to put Al-Arian and his alleged jihadists in prison for the rest of their lives.

Prominent Muslim leaders have been warning the U.S. government and the public for years about such groups. Sheik Muhammad Hisham Kabbani, chairman of the Detroit-based Supreme Council of America and part of a respected family of traditional Islamic scholars that has led the muftiate of Lebanon for the last 150 years. Kabbani has been warning about the jihadist groups since 1996. "I saw there was a danger," he tells *Insight*. "Many Muslims in the United States were aware of the danger, but they didn't have the capacity to speak on behalf of the Muslim community because the microphone has been hijacked."

> *Terrorists and their supporters are doing their best to weave themselves into the political fabric of American society.*

Al-Arian says his indictment and arrest simply are the result of "politics." The AMC, in a joint statement with other groups claiming to represent the American Muslim community, echoed Al-Arian: "The community is gaining the perception that people are rounded up and targeted because of their political opinions and because they have the right to dissent on current U.S. policy. Our community is in dire need to understand how these charges are founded on concrete evidence of crimi-

nal activity and not guilt by association or political considera-
tions." Not showing the slightest bit of caution about the terrorist conspiracy alleged in the indictments, the AMC turned
its ire on the Bush administration, particularly Attorney General John Ashcroft.

A Long History of Supporting Terrorism

Since 9/11 the AMC and affiliated groups have portrayed American Muslims as victims of U.S. bigotry rather than partners in
the fight against terrorism. And that, critics say, has helped to
tarnish the public image of Muslims and Arab-Americans as
unpatriotic or even pro-terrorist. An ongoing *Insight* investigation, which began within hours of the hijacked jetliners crash-
ing into the World Trade Center, the Pentagon and a field in
Pennsylvania, shows that many of the groups the Bush administration has courted have resisted the Bush dictum, "You're either with us or you're with the terrorists." Those groups appear
to want to have it both ways, condemning terrorism in general
and wrapping themselves in the American flag, Constitution in
hand, while at the same time extending political, moral, material or other support to international terrorists and assailing the
Bush administration and federal law-enforcement agencies
charged with waging the war on terror.

> *Since 9/11 the [American Muslim Council]
> and affiliated groups have portrayed American
> Muslims as victims of U.S. bigotry rather than
> partners in the fight against terrorism.*

Angrily denying that it supports terrorism, the AMC claims
to be "fully engaged" with the U.S. government in the antiterrorism fight. Communications director Faiz Rehman claims allegations that the AMC has a history hostile to Bush's war on
terrorism are "blatantly false."

The AMC was founded in 1990 by Abdurahman Alamoudi,
a veteran operative for Saudi-backed political-action organizations, including the SAAR [Sulaiman Abdul Aziz al-Rajhi] Foundation, which was raided by federal agents for alleged terrorist
financing. According to national-security specialists, the AMC

has a long and consistent history in the United States of promoting terrorist causes or linked groups—many of which are unrelated to Islam or to the Arab-Israeli conflict. An early president of the executive board of the AMC was Jamil Abdullah Al-Amin, formerly known as H. Rap Brown, who was twice on the FBI's Ten Most Wanted list. As a 1960s radical, Brown threatened to assassinate Lady Bird Johnson when she was first lady of the United States. He now is serving a life sentence in a Georgia prison for the 2000 murder of Fulton County Sheriff's Deputy Ricky Kinchen.

> *The [American Muslim Council] has a long and consistent history in the United States of promoting terrorist causes or linked groups.*

As AMC executive director, both on CNN's *Crossfire* and in an open letter, Alamoudi defended Egyptian Islamic Jihad spiritual leader Omar Abdel Rahman, the "Blind Sheik" convicted of masterminding the 1993 World Trade Center bombing in New York City. In its April 1994 newsletter, AMC defended the ruling Sudanese National Islamic Front, which the State Department designated as a terrorist group, arguing that the Khartoum regime was "not engaged in terrorist activities and is not harboring terrorists." At its 1997 conference, the AMC played host to Layth Shubayalat, alleged to be a terrorist tied to a plot to assassinate King Hussein of Jordan, and defended the outlawed Jordanian Islamic Action Front.

Demonstrating in front of the White House in 2000, Alamoudi was videotaped proclaiming: "We are all supporters of Hamas [terrorist group]. Allahu Akbar! I am also a supporter of Hezbollah [terrorist group]." Among the most infamous attacks officially attributed to Hezbollah are the April 1983 bombing of the American Embassy in Beirut, Lebanon, which killed 63, and the October 1983 truck bombing of the U.S. Marine barracks in Beirut, which killed 241 Marines.

Alamoudi recruited young, articulate, personable Muslim political activists and helped them set up spin-off groups to influence the political mainstream. Canceled checks obtained by *Insight* show that he provided seed money for one of those groups, the Islamic Institute, which his former government-affairs director, Khaled Saffuri, co-founded with conservative activist Grover Norquist. Saffuri was involved in Muslim outreach for the 2000 Bush campaign and currently serves as chairman of the Islamic Institute. He has told *Insight* he opposes groups such as Hamas and Hezbollah.

The Political Goals of the AMC

Critics claim the AMC's main political activity has been to abolish or prevent passage of antiterrorist legislation. The AMC calls itself an "active member" of the National Coalition to Protect Political Freedom (NCPPF), which was founded in the 1960s to provide legal support to New Left terrorists in the Weather Underground, the Puerto Rican FALN[1] and the Black Liberation Army, and which national-security specialists say was revived to push for Islamist terrorist causes.

NCPPF Executive Director Kit Gage is a veteran legal activist, serving also as head of the National Lawyers Guild, founded in the 1930s and officially cited as a legal front group for the old Communist Party. The NCPPF has acted as a legal-aid office of sorts for members or alleged members of a wide variety of terrorist groups . . . including the Popular Front for the Liberation of Palestine, the Egyptian Islamic Jihad, Hamas, the Basque ETA[2] separatist group of Spain, the FALN of Puerto Rico, the Provisional Irish Republican Army and the Shining Path of Peru, and for Leonard Peltier, who was convicted of the 1975 murders of FBI Special Agents Jack Coler and Ronald Williams.

From 2000 to 2002, the NCPPF president was USF professor Sami Al-Arian. And here is where the alleged Palestinian Islamic Jihad leader, whom the FBI considers a hard-core, senior terrorist, comes publicly under the AMC's wing and into the White House.

The AMC began to enter the political mainstream during the 2000 presidential campaign. Some Republican activists seized on the secret-evidence issue to woo Muslim and Arab-American voters. The AMC's annual convention, held in June, 2000, was devoted to the task of influencing Congress. Alamoudi presided as convention chairman. June 22 was designated "Muslim Day on the Hill," with seminars in lobbying held in

1. Fuerzas Armada Liberacion Nacional Puertoriquena, or the Armed Forces of Puerto Rican National Liberation   2. Euzkadi Ta Askatasuna, or Basque Fatherland and Liberty

the Cannon House Office Building of the U.S. House of Representatives. The first lobbying coach, according to the program, was Al-Arian, identified as being with the Tampa Bay Coalition for Peace and Justice. Gage of the NCPPF "provided information on secret evidence" as part of a "campaign to support the Secret Evidence Repeal Act of 2001," according to the AMC's newsletter, *AMC Report*. A Capitol Hill dinner that night presented awards to Reps. Tom Davis (R-Va.) and John Conyers (D-Mich.), Islamic Institute cofounder Norquist, identified as president of Americans for Tax Reform, and James Zogby, president of the Arab-American Institute.

The 2001 Conference

Al-Arian was back at the AMC's 2001 conference, held in Northern Virginia, from June 21–24. He again kicked off the legislative-action session. "Sami Al-Arian, president of the National Coalition to Protect Political Freedom (NCPPF), spoke about secret evidence," the AMC newsletter reported. Following Al-Arian's presentation was a session called "Art of Lobbying." Indeed, "Suhail Khan, [at the time] representing the White House Office of Public Liaison, addressed the members on how to be successful in lobbying," the newsletter continued. "According to Khan, another important aspect of lobbying is facilitating meetings with congressional staffers." Coached by Al-Arian and Khan in two separate panels, the AMC delegates spent the rest of the day lobbying.

> *Critics claim the [American Muslim Council's] main political activity has been to abolish or prevent passage of antiterrorist legislation.*

"The second day's biggest event was 'The White House Briefing' with Karl Rove, President [George W.] Bush's senior political adviser, who welcomed the participants and gave them the orientation of Bush's agenda followed by a brief question-and-answer session," the AMC reported. (Al-Arian was part of the AMC delegation, his wife, Nahla, stated at a news conference. *Newsweek* reports that the Secret Service warned White House political officials that Al-Arian was a suspected terrorist and that he should not be cleared, but that political officials let him in anyway. In the days following Al-Arian's arrest, according to Washington-based journalists, White House officials initially denied to reporters that Rove had participated in the event, but later changed their story.)

At the 2001 convention's kickoff luncheon, "Alamoudi gave the opening remarks and introduced Suhail Khan, who received an award for his contributions of work concerning the rights of Muslims," according to the AMC Report. The newsletter added that the AMC then ratified Alamoudi's work of the previous decade, with an officer reminding the audience "of the great role Alamoudi played in establishing and leading AMC from the days of its inception until what it is today."

Khan has said that while he has met Al-Arian he has had no personal relationship with the suspected terrorist leader. He also has strongly condemned Alamoudi and people like him.

The FBI and the AMC

The AMC and related groups firmly deny any and all allegations that they are soft on terrorism. In a strongly worded response to critics, dated Feb. 20, AMC's Rehman says, "While the AMC may have differences on certain domestic- and international-policy issues with the Bush administration, FBI Director Robert Mueller was [2001's] keynote speaker at the AMC's annual convention, which is a testimony to the organization's support to the administration on the matters of national security."

Not so, say administration insiders, who tell *Insight* that Mueller was instructed to address the AMC under political pressure from the White House. Administration officials tell this magazine that a bitter controversy erupted within the National Security Council in an effort to prevent Mueller from addressing the AMC at its June 2002 convention. Widespread but unconfirmed suspicions led to White House political operatives who wanted to assuage Muslim groups alarmed by Bush's strong antiterrorist measures after 9/11. The government's public position was awkward. FBI spokesman Bill Carter defended the AMC as "the most mainstream Muslim group in the country," but the FBI media unit could produce nothing to substantiate the claim.

In his speech, which was aimed at the Muslim and Arab-American community at large, the FBI director broke with protocol and did not recognize his AMC hosts by name or praise or credit the organization. Mueller's only reference to the AMC was this: "Unfortunately, persons associated with this organization have in the past made statements that indicate support for terrorism and for terrorist organizations."

> **"** *[American Muslim Council] executive director [Eric E.] Vickers, when requested to do so in four separate interviews on Fox News and MSNBC in June 2002, would not denounce Hamas, Hezbollah or even al-Qaeda by name.* **"**

The FBI chief credited AMC President Yahya Basha as an individual for firmly condemning terrorism, but he ignored the controversial televised statements during the previous week by Executive Director Eric E. Vickers, who would not denounce Hamas, Hezbollah, or al-Qaeda [terrorist group] by name when asked by Fox News and MSNBC. . . . While Mueller strongly praised "the American Muslim community" at large for providing vital support to the FBI in ongoing antiterrorism efforts, his silence about the AMC itself was taken by close observers to reflect the break between the vocal Washington-based Muslim groups and the American Muslim rank and file.

Not True Allies of the FBI

Even so, the AMC has been milking the FBI director's appearance at its convention as confirmation of its legitimacy. The AMC and other groups, such as the spin-off Islamic Institute, have cast themselves as allies of the FBI in the war against terrorism since 9/11. The AMC recently blasted syndicated columnist Mona Charen for writing that the group after Sept. 11 had encouraged its members not to talk to the FBI. "This is far from the truth," the AMC's Rehman says in a written rebuttal. "In fact, on Sept. 17, 2001, AMC issued a statement urging Muslims to assist [the] FBI. This press release has been present on the front page of our Website since that date."

But the evidence shows that Charen essentially was correct. Until Sept. 27, 2001, the AMC Website included a page urging support of the Secret Evidence Repeal Act, stating that it eliminates the use of secret information in immigration proceedings. "AMC has contacted every member of Congress. . . . We ask you to do the same." The last sentence was in bold type and hyperlinked to an NCPPF site which instructed readers on how to avoid cooperation with the FBI or other law-enforcement officers in antiterrorism cases. The instructions are titled "Know Your Rights: Don't Talk to the FBI." The site as of that date—more than two weeks after the al-Qaeda attacks [on September 11]—contained nothing urging Muslims to assist federal officials.

Insight's monitoring of the AMC Website shows that the council did not pull the anti-FBI material until after coming under heavy criticism for failing to mobilize its members to help federal counterterrorism investigators. The "statement urging Muslims to assist FBI," though dated Sept. 17, was not posted on the AMC site for at least another 10 days. Even then, the statement did nothing to encourage anyone to work with the FBI to root out terrorist supporters and operatives from Islamic centers, mosques and other institutions within the Muslim community. It merely urged them to seek service, for pay, as translators—historically a favored posting for operatives and agents. Other radical jihadist activist groups purged their Websites of anti-FBI material at about the same time.

Continued Opposition to Antiterrorism Efforts

The legislative track record against antiterrorist legislation is consistent both before and after 9/11. The AMC opposed the 1996 Anti-Terrorism and Effective Death Penalty Act, according to its October 1995 newsletter. It lobbied for the Secret Evidence Repeal Act two years in a row "to raise the concerns of American Muslims on the infringement of their constitutional rights," according to its Website. In concert with the GOP-oriented Islamic Institute, the AMC lobbied post-9/11 against key provisions of the 2001 USA PATRIOT Act, the Bush administration's legislative package of new legal tools to defend the country against terrorism, and called for the resignation of Attorney General Ashcroft. In a June 14, 2002, statement titled "AMC Charges Ashcroft With Engagement in Scare Tactics as Pretext to Curtail Civil Liberties," the group accused the attorney general of "using national security as a pretext" to "engage in a pattern of ethnic and religious discrimination" and "intimidation." In February [2003], the AMC posted notice that it will fight the administration's proposed Domestic Security Enhancement Act of 2003.[3]

Rather than praise the Justice Department for helping cleanse the Muslim community of terrorist operatives out to attack all Americans, as many had hoped, the AMC attacked Ashcroft in a joint statement with the Council on American Islamic Relations, the American Muslim Alliance (founded by its president, Agha Saeed, the former chairman of the Communist Party of Pakistan) and the Muslim Public Affairs Council. In a bizarre document disregarding the widely known facts concerning the attacks of Sept. 11 and showing a surprising ignorance of American jurisprudence, the statement said: "It was disturbing that Attorney General John Ashcroft inserted expressions, like jihad and martyrdom, to a major federal investigation and indictment."

The AMC and allied groups say they have "repeatedly and unconditionally condemned violence and suicide bombings," in Rehman's words. "Our Website still carries these statements clearly outlining our position on these matters." True enough. But it won't name the perpetrators. While its president and public-relations people offer a moderate image, the day-to-day leadership shows where the organization's heart is, a growing number of critics say. For example, executive director Vickers, when requested to do so in four separate interviews on Fox News and MSNBC in June 2002, would not denounce Hamas, Hezbollah or even al-Qaeda by name. Linda Vester of Fox News asked Vickers, "Do you condemn al-Qaeda by name and condemn Hamas by name?" According to the transcript, Vickers would not.

Journalists Fred Barnes and Morton Kondracke, in a panel with Fox anchor Brit Hume, discussed the AMC executive director's comments. Barnes commented, "These groups are outraged about what the victims are doing here in the United States. Their big effort is to oppose reasonable steps to protect the United States from further attacks. That's where they aim their fire, not at these terrorists who are doing this in the name of their very own religion." Kondracke added, "If that guy truly reflects American Muslims—and he is the executive director of this large organization—then God help us. We've got . . . that guy sounds like a fifth column, frankly."

3. This is a proposed sequel to the Patriot Act that as of spring 2005 had not been approved by Congress.

4

American Muslims Do Not Support Terrorist Groups

John Tirman

John Tirman is the executive director of the Center for International Studies at the Massachusetts Institute of Technology, and the coauthor and editor of The Maze of Fear: Security and Migration After 9/11.

Despite the fears that arose in the wake of the September 11, 2001, terrorist attacks on New York City and Washington, D.C., American Muslims have not provided a social base for the al Qaeda terror network, the organization that orchestrated the attacks. While al Qaeda may have operatives living in the United States, it is unlikely that they have any connections to local Islamic communities.

O ne of the mysteries surrounding the September 11, 2001, terrorist attacks and the frequent terrorist alerts ever since is the role played, if any, by American Muslims in supporting al-Qaeda operations. The U.S. government acts as if there is a support base of some kind. White House Chief of Staff Andrew Card told a CNN reporter during the Republican convention, "We know there are al-Qaeda cells" operating inside the country. During the early August [2004] scare about terrorists targeting financial institutions, newspaper reports often alluded to, but did not identify or describe, a support network of individuals living in the United States.

John Tirman, "Mistrusted Muslims: Investigations of U.S. Muslims Turn Up Little Terror," *National Catholic Reporter*, vol. 41, January 14, 2005. Copyright © 2005 by *National Catholic Reporter*, www.natcath.org. Reproduced by permission of the publisher and the author.

For the 5 million or so Muslims in the United States, a large majority of whom are U.S. citizens, such implications are troubling. Their communities across the country have been shaken by the post-9/11 antiterrorist campaign: Law enforcement agents have interviewed nearly 200,000 Muslims and others from predominantly Muslim countries; hundreds have been deported or detained for long periods; thousands were subject to a "special registration," and now some hundreds have been indicted in widely publicized "terrorist" prosecutions. Charities and other social institutions have been shut down or disabled, and surveillance in these communities is now a given. But the cardinal question of whether or not domestic Muslim populations actually pose a security threat remains unanswered, indeed, unarticulated, in public discourse and official pronouncements.

The Nexus of Threat

The question is neither impolite nor unimportant. We know that most politically violent groups require a "social base"—clusters of knowing supporters who do not participate directly in militant operations. Such a social base is likely to exist where such groups are hiding and where they carry out attacks. Diasporas often support such groups with money, communications and political access. None of this is particularly new, but before 9/11 the violence was always somewhere else—Northern Ireland, Palestine, South Africa and the like—and not in America.

> **Muslims living in America have not constituted a social base for al-Qaeda.**

Now the nexus of threat is here, and the rules of the game are altered. There is no territorial struggle, and the numbers of ethnic and national populations involved number two dozen or more. International migration has created enormous flows of people, including many thousands of new immigrants seeking work every year. Muslims, like many immigrant waves before them, tend to gravitate toward each other into neighborhoods where mosques, common language, social networks and opportunities exist.

It is these communities in Brooklyn, New Jersey, Detroit,

Los Angeles, Chicago and elsewhere that have attracted the attention of law enforcement officials. Are radical imams [religious leaders] preaching violence against America? Are Quranic schools training future terrorists? Are charities really supporting al-Qaeda or Hamas or Chechen murderers? Most Americans would probably consider these as legitimate concerns in the wake of the 9/11 atrocities.

No Evidence of Terror Cells

The evidence thus far, however, indicates that Muslims living in America have not constituted a social base for al-Qaeda. It is striking, in fact, that so little illegality has been uncovered in a population so thoroughly investigated and watched. The prosecutions of alleged terrorist-related activities, which should represent the most definitive picture of how the government views the internal threat, have established very little—if anything—that could be described as evidence of al-Qaeda cells operating in the United States. Nothing else in the publicly known record of this massive law enforcement and intelligence effort suggests that a conspiracy exists, a remarkably clean bill for these communities.

> *The great danger here is that over years of suspicion, innuendo and harassment . . . Muslims in America will feel increasing isolation and hostility.*

Notably, the 9/11 Commission itself found no evidence of a domestic social base prior to 9/11 that was knowingly aiding the hijackers. Some of the 19 conspirators received some minor assistance from an individual or two, but those individuals have not been identified, described or prosecuted; if they existed, they may also have been here, like the attackers, on temporary visas from Saudi Arabia or elsewhere. They were very likely not rooted in local communities, and indeed the hijackers stayed clear of such attachments as well. If al-Qaeda did not have such a support base in the United States prior to the attacks, it is even less likely they have one now. That does not mean there are no operatives here; they could, like the 9/11 cabal, sneak into the country and keep to themselves. But the supposition of many in the U.S. government is that American Muslim communities are likely to harbor, support or perhaps even initiate terrorism.

New Fears for Muslims

This suspicion is rocking these very communities in ways that not only challenge their civil liberties but also may be counterproductive in numerous ways.

One of the first victims of the post-9/11 climate of fear in Muslim and Arab-American communities is charitable giving. Support for both Palestinians and for victims of the U.S. occupation of Iraq is now considered precarious. Material support—donations through charities, most prominently—is especially hazardous because so many of these institutions have been targeted by law enforcement officials as terrorist related. More nonpolitical philanthropy is also drying up because of the fear that appearing on any such list creates vulnerabilities for the donor.

Speech is constrained, often self-censored, but now, too, by Washington's actions. The recent denial of a work visa for Muslim philosopher Tariq Ramadan, an inspirational professor who was to teach at Notre Dame, sends a signal that moderate voices will be excluded. In surveys, interviews and meetings of Muslims and Arab-Americans, they describe strong feelings of isolation and alienation from the American mainstream, disrespect for their views on the wars in Iraq and Afghanistan as well as the Palestinian question, and a sense of hopelessness about finding a place for Islam in American society. At a gathering of national and local leaders of Muslim and Arab-American communities at the Social Science Research Council in Washington [in fall 2004], a few spoke openly of internment should another act of terrorism befall America.

All of this turmoil has its consequences. It can scarcely come as a surprise that in surveys in the Muslim world, even in friendly places like Turkey and Jordan, the United States is viewed as a menace, at war with Islam. The treatment of Muslims in the United States is one element of those perceptions. The great danger here is that over years of suspicion, innuendo and harassment, buttressed by a new culture of internal security, Muslims in America will feel increasing isolation and hostility, beyond even what they sense nowadays. Among their youth, this could even result in a strain of radicalism. Thus, for this new national security state, a new security dilemma—its creation of the forces it fears, certainly abroad and possibly now even at home, where no such force existed. But even the less alarming consequences, the palpable sense of fear and exclusion from American society, are a travesty of justice and fair play. We need in all our institutions—law enforcement, news media, education, businesses and others—a commitment to holding innocent what is not proven guilty and welcoming these communities as a growing part of America's dreamland of rich diversity.

5

American Muslims Have Played a Key Role in the Fight Against Terrorism

Robert S. Mueller III

Robert S. Mueller III is a former director of the Federal Bureau of Investigation.

Muslim Americans were especially affected by the September 11, 2001, terrorist attacks. They have been wrongly targeted because they belong to the same religion as the terrorists. Despite being treated unfairly, Muslim Americans have been willing to step forward and help the FBI in its fight against terrorism. They have provided valuable services such as translating, interviewing prisoners, and teaching FBI agents about Muslim beliefs and practices. However, in order for Muslim Americans to effectively contribute to antiterrorism efforts, they must not allow some Muslims to speak out in favor of terrorism.

Editor's Note: The following viewpoint was originally given as a speech to the annual conference of the American Muslim Council on June 28, 2002.

Thank you, Dr. [Yahya] Basha [president of the American Muslim Council], for the introduction, and good afternoon everyone. I appreciate the invitation to talk with you today, to talk to you about the relationship of the FBI with the American Muslim community. I am here because we must all be in this

Robert S. Mueller III, "American Muslims: All Americans Pulling Together," *Vital Speeches of the Day*, vol. 68, July 15, 2002, p. 580.

war against terrorism together and because a sound and trusting relationship with the Muslim community can only bear the fruit of a safer nation for us all. I appreciate the help and support many in the American Muslim communities have already given us, especially over the past nine months, and I call on you, as Americans, to continue working with us to defeat terror. As we all know, it will be a long and difficult struggle.

Muslim Americans Have Suffered

I realize that like all Americans, Muslim Americans have been deeply impacted by the [September 11, 2001, terrorist attacks]. You lost family, friends and fellow Muslims that day.

And I know that the American Muslim community has suffered in other ways from the events of September 11. Sadly, some individuals in this country have questioned the loyalty of some Muslim Americans to this country just because of their race and religion. In some cases, American Muslims have been targets of discrimination and hateful words. Some houses of worship have been damaged and desecrated. A number of Muslim Americans—and others wrongly believed to be Muslims—have been threatened, attacked, and even killed. These attacks against you and your communities are not only reprehensible, like terrorism, they are attacks against humanity. At a time like this, when you are vulnerable, it is important that you have access to your government. That is why, within hours of the attacks, the FBI opened a dialogue with many Muslim and Arab-American organizations. This is not the first time we have worked together; we have had a productive and beneficial relationship with the members of your community for several years. But we did come together with a new sense of urgency. We were told of concerns about retaliatory attacks in your communities in the wake of the terrorist hijackings, and we in the FBI promised to do something about it.

In response to your concerns, the President, the Attorney General, and I all emphatically stressed that such attacks would not be tolerated and would be prosecuted to the fullest extent of the law. And we followed through on that commitment. In the days following September 11, the FBI investigated numerous attacks and threats against Arab-, Muslim-, and Sikh-Americans. In all, we have launched more than 360 investigations in concert with state and local law enforcement. Well over 100 individuals have already been charged with federal,

40

state, and local crimes. Fortunately, the number of retaliatory assaults dropped off quickly, but our commitment to aggressive investigations remains as strong as ever. And we appreciate all the support your communities and others have given us in identifying victims and bringing to justice those who have committed these terrible acts.

Muslim Americans Have Supported the FBI

Even as we have investigated these hate crimes, we in the FBI have continued to build our relationships with the American Muslim community in other areas. Shortly after the attacks, and again in February [2002], I met personally with a number of American Muslim leaders to discuss our September 11 investigation and to hear their thoughts and concerns. In September, we also asked our 56 field offices to reach out to Muslim Americans in their communities, to address your concerns, to build relationships, and to ask once again for help.

As I prepared to talk with you today, I asked our Special Agents in Charge to update me on the steps they had taken. Their response was overwhelming. They wrote back with story after story of productive meetings, insights, generosity, and substantive assistance. In all, our field offices attended more than 500 meetings and made some 6,000 personal contacts in Muslim and Arab American communities. They went to mosques, town halls, and media briefings. They held recruiting drives. They invited—and graduated—members of Muslim communities at FBI Citizens' Academies.

> *Many in the American Muslim community have come forward to support the FBI in very visible ways.*

At the same time, many in the American Muslim community have come forward to support the FBI in very visible ways. Many leaders have generously sent educational materials to our field offices and to our headquarters. They have taken the time to talk with our Agents and support professionals to help them better understand Muslim perspectives and Muslim beliefs. Muslim Americans have cooperated with our interviews and supported our investigations. In some cases, Arab-American newspapers have even provided us with useful information. The active work of many in the American Muslim community in cities nationwide has merited public thanks and praise. But perhaps the greatest act of support has been the way Muslim- and Arab-Americans have responded to our urgent need for translators. Six days after September 11, I announced that the FBI was seeking Arabic and Farsi language experts. The response was extraordinary. Within hours, our switchboard was overwhelmed with calls. Those who came forward included doctors, lawyers, engineers, academics— Muslim- and Arab-Americans from all walks of life who were willing to quit their jobs, come to work for the FBI, and give something back to their country in the fight against terrorism.

As a result, we have doubled our number of Arabic translators and linguists, and many more candidates are in the process of being hired. Already, these language experts have made important contributions. They have helped us substantially reduce the backlog of materials needing to be translated. They have gone to Guantanamo Bay [Cuba, where a U.S. detention center for suspected terrorists is located] to help us interview prisoners. They have supported our FBI offices around the world. Again, I want to thank the many Muslim-Americans who have provided help to the FBI [since September 2001.] It has been invaluable. At the same time, I ask you again in the strongest of terms for your continued support. Because the reality is, we need it more than ever. Make no mistake about it, our country remains vulnerable to attack. Day after day, intelligence about potential attacks continues to pour in from across the globe, prompting warnings and keeping our nation in a permanent state of alert. Time after time, Al Qaeda [terrorist group] has openly threatened America, saying more attacks are on the way.

Preventing Further Terrorism

The President has asked the FBI to do everything in its power— within the bounds of the Constitution—to prevent the next attack in concert with our partners in the law enforcement and intelligence communities. We are fully committed to doing so. But it is no easy task. Our society is so open, our population so large, our landmarks so plentiful, and our borders so extensive. We must head off attacks and track down terrorists and those who support terrorism in our own cities and neighborhoods, and we must also be there to help every nation where America has a presence and every country where terrorism has put down roots.

To prevent terrorism we must have: excellent intelligence work; superior analytic capability; robust investigations; state-of-the-art technology, seamless partnerships; and the strong support of the people—all people. The FBI is racing to improve in every one of those areas, and that is driving what is perhaps the most fundamental transformation in our history. We have restructured our Headquarters. We have created a range of prevention programs that simply didn't exist before September 11, and refocused many that did. With nearly half-a-billion dollars in funds from Congress, we are overhauling our technology as quickly as we can given how far behind current capabilities we are today. To vastly improve our ability to manage and analyze information, we are hiring a crop of new analysts, borrowing resources from agencies like the CIA, and improving the skills of those on board. And we are rethinking and rebuilding relationships with a range of organizations and agencies, including our 650,000 colleagues in law enforcement nationwide.

All of this is putting a tremendous strain on the men and women of the FBI. They are working long hours, missing dinners and soccer games and birthdays, all so that they don't miss that one lead that might prevent the next attack. They are changing how they do things in mid-stream, adjusting to a vast array of changes in their operations. They are reaching out to their many colleagues, coordinating with every agency under the sun, in ways they have never done before.

It is clear, however, that the men and women of the FBI can't do it all alone. The Bureau has 11,000 Agents, about one quarter of New York City's police force.

Educating the FBI

We are one nation, and we are all in this together. The FBI needs the support not just of its law enforcement and intelligence partners; we need the support of every person within our borders. There is no question that all of you can help. You can help us better understand your communities and the concerns of those who live in them. You can help by telling us about suspicious behavior, as thousands of Americans have done since September 11. You can help by staying alert wherever you might be, like the courageous flight attendants and passengers who foiled the "shoe bomber" over the waters of the Atlantic. Most especially, you can help by working to overcome the differences that separate us all, the dividing lines of beliefs and culture that incite terrorism and support for terrorism.

> *Like all Americans, [Muslims] were shocked and outraged by the terrorist hijackings and quickly condemned them.*

We also need help educating our Agents in dealing with Muslim communities here and around the world. The more culturally fluent our investigators are, the more effective and respectful our investigations will be. For some time, the FBI has incorporated ethics and cultural diversity into new Agent training and continuing education programs for all Bureau employees. But we need to do more. And you can help us do so. Let me give an example. Almost a year before the attacks of September 11 an Agent from our Atlanta Field Office went to interview two women originally from Afghanistan. The interview went well. The Agent handled himself professionally, and he treated both of these individuals with respect and courtesy. But he later found out that he had inadvertently violated Afghan culture by sitting down in the home of these two women without an Afghan adult male present. Later that day, two Agents and four Afghan representatives met over dinner to bridge the gap of differences. Everyone came away with a better understanding of each other's concerns and perspectives. That dinner was a success and the ultimate result was an FBI program called "Bridging the Gap" that is raising awareness and understanding among Atlanta immigrants in concert with a local project of the same name.

Now, let me fast forward to just this month [June 2002]. In the first week in June, we held a four-day training conference for FBI managers. As part of that training, we brought in a panel of diverse speakers, including a local Imam who articulated the viewpoints and concerns of the Muslim-American community. And this past Tuesday, Dr. Aziza Al-Hibri was kind enough to participate in a nationwide satellite broadcast on Arab-American and Islamic Cultural Awareness for FBI investigators, our multiagency Joint Terrorism Task Forces and U.S. Attorneys.

In the months to come, we have still more plans underway. Next month, we will begin a national program to begin counter-terrorism training for every member of our many Joint Terrorist Task Forces, including at least four hours on the tenets and cultures of Islam. We're also expanding similar training for new and current Agents.

Speaking with One Voice

As I finish, I would like to return for a moment to the impact of the events of September 11th, to the importance of building a relationship between the Muslim community and the FBI, and to issues that may strain our best intentions in that regard. As I am sure you are aware, my appearance here today has generated some controversy. And while that did not deter me from coming, as with most such matters I believe it is best to address it openly. My reason for being here is simple: to continue our discussion and help build a relationship that I am convinced is beneficial to us all. But I think it is also important to be open and frank about the concerns of those who urged me not to attend.

> *We in the FBI need to do our part, and we are counting on the American Muslim community to do its part.*

Like all Americans, you were shocked and outraged by the terrorist hijackings and quickly condemned them. As Dr. Basha has said, echoing sentiments across the nation, Muslim-Americans felt violated by the attacks, and he wasted no time in denouncing those horrible acts in the strongest language possible.

Nonetheless, you have not always spoken with one voice. Unfortunately, persons associated with this organization have in the past made statements that indicate support for terrorism and for terrorist organizations. I think we can—Muslims and non-Muslim alike—justifiably be outraged by such statements. No perceived political or other agenda justifies acts of terrorism. We must be, as Dr. Basha is, loud in our condemnation of acts of terrorism.

We must—again, together—speak out against terrorism, and

—again, together—act to thwart terrorism. As we move forward into the future, what's clear is that we are operating in a different and dangerous environment, one that requires all of us to be more aware and more diligent when it comes to our security. America has always been a land of diversity, a nation rich in ethnic and cultural chemistry. But what has always seen us through the tough times is our unity. All through history, Americans have found a way to put aside their differences and to step forward with courage in times of need.

World War II was such a time, and there are many examples of Americans who overcame years of adversity to make a profound difference for the future. Like the Tuskegee Airmen, a group of courageous and spirited African-Americans, who battled discrimination long before they took on the enemy in the skies of Europe. Like the Navajo Indians who, with their beautiful and sophisticated native language nearing extinction, created a code for the Marines in the Pacific Theater, a code that could never be cracked.

Today, America faces a new, potentially more dangerous global conflict. The threat is elusive, with ever shifting terrorist tactics and enemies who are nearly invisible. The weapons are instruments of terror: from explosive-laden vehicles to "dirty bombs." And the front lines are right here at home, in our own streets and cities and neighborhoods. We need to pull together as a nation. We in the FBI need to do our part, and we are counting on the American Muslim community to do its part. I look forward to working with members of your community in the weeks and months ahead. Thank you very much.

6

The Civil Rights of Arab American Muslims Are Being Violated

James J. Zogby

James J. Zogby is the president of the Arab American Institute.

The terrorist attacks of September 11, 2001, were a great tragedy for all Americans, including Arab Americans. However, because the nineteen terrorists who hijacked the four planes were Middle Eastern Muslims, Arab Americans were suddenly viewed with suspicion and became the targets of discrimination and hate crimes. Moreover, the Patriot Act and other counterterrorism measures have threatened the civil liberties of Arab and Muslim immigrants who have been detained as part of the September 11 investigations. These detainees, despite having no connection to terrorists, have been treated poorly in the detention centers. Other efforts by the Department of Justice to reduce terrorism, including interviewing Arab and Muslim immigrants and citizens, have led to workplace discrimination and created fear in the Arab American community. By singling out the Arab American Muslim community, the U.S. government is harming its relationship with Arabs worldwide.

Editor's Note: The following viewpoint was originally given as a statement before the U.S. Senate on November 18, 2003.

M r. Chairman [Utah senator Orrin Hatch], Ranking Member, Members of the Committee, thank you for convening this

James J. Zogby, statement before the U.S. Senate Committee on the Judiciary, Washington, DC, November 18, 2003.

important hearing and for inviting me to be with you today.

The horrific terrorist attacks of September 11 [2001] were a profound and painful tragedy for all Americans. None of us will ever forget that awful day when thousands of innocent lives were lost.

A Backlash Against Arab Americans

The attacks were a dual tragedy for Arab Americans. We are Americans and it was our country that was attacked. Arab Americans died in the attacks. Arab Americans were also part of the rescue effort. Dozens of New York City Police and rescue workers who bravely toiled at Ground Zero were Arab Americans.

> *Many Arab Americans were torn away from mourning [the September 11, 2001, terrorist attacks] with our fellow Americans because we became the targets of hate crimes and discrimination.*

Sadly, however, many Arab Americans were torn away from mourning with our fellow Americans because we became the targets of hate crimes and discrimination. Some assumed our collective guilt because the terrorists were Arabs. Arab Americans and Muslims and others perceived to be Arab and Muslim were the victims of hundreds of bias incidents. According to the Justice Department's Civil Rights Division, "The incidents have consisted of telephone, internet, mail, and face-to-face threats; minor assaults as well as assaults with dangerous weapons and assaults resulting in serious injury and death; and vandalism, shootings, and bombings directed at homes, businesses, and places of worship." As a result of the post-9/11 backlash, in 2001, the FBI reported a 1600% increase in anti-Muslim hate crimes and an almost 500% increase in ethnic-based hate crimes against persons of Arab descent.

Thankfully, the American people rallied to our defense. President [George W.] Bush spoke out forcefully against hate crimes, as did countless others across the nation. Both the Senate and the House of Representatives unanimously passed resolutions condemning hate crimes against Arab Americans and

Muslims. Federal, state and local law enforcement investigated and prosecuted hate crimes, and ordinary citizens defended and protected us, refusing to allow bigots to define America. We will always be grateful that our fellow Americans defended us at that crucial time.

Arab Americans Have Helped Fight Terrorism

Much has been done in the past two years to combat the threat of terrorism. Among other significant accomplishments, we have deposed the Taliban regime [which ruled Afghanistan], created the Department of Homeland Security, taken steps to enhance airport and border security, and improved information sharing between intelligence and law enforcement.

Arab Americans are proud to have played a crucial role in these efforts, serving on the front lines of the war on terrorism as police, firefighters, soldiers, FBI agents, and translators. The Arab American Institute has worked with federal, state and local law enforcement to assist efforts to protect the homeland. We helped to recruit Arab Americans with needed language skills and we have served as a bridge to connect law enforcement with our community.

Recently, working with the Washington Field Office of the FBI, the Arab American Institute helped to create the first Arab American Advisory Committee, which works to facilitate communications between the Arab-American community and the FBI. I proudly serve as a member of the FBI Advisory Committee, which serves as a model and is now being copied across the United States.

Questionable Measures

As someone who has spent my entire professional life working to bring Arab Americans into the mainstream of American political life and to build a bridge between my country and the Arab world, I am very concerned about the direction of some of our efforts to combat the terrorist threat and the impact these initiatives have on our country and my community. Unfortunately, the Bush administration has devoted too many resources to counterterrorism measures that threaten our civil liberties and do little to improve our security. Going well beyond the provisions of the Patriot Act, [Attorney General] John Ashcroft's Justice Department [DOJ] has unleashed a series of high-profile initiatives that explicitly target Arabs and Muslims and have resulted in the detention of thousands of people.

In the immediate aftermath of 9/11, the Justice Department rounded up at least 1200 immigrants, the vast majority of whom were Arab or Muslim. The DOJ refused to release any information about the detainees, and charged that the detentions were related to the 9/11 investigation. At the time, the Arab American Institute and others in the Arab-American community expressed concern about the broad dragnet that the Justice Department had cast in Arab immigrant communities. We fully supported the government's efforts to investigate the 9/11 terrorist attacks, but we questioned the efficacy of this dragnet approach. . . .

> *The Bush administration has devoted too many resources to counterterrorism measures that threaten our civil liberties.*

[In 2002], the Justice Department's Inspector General [IG] issued a report that vindicated our concerns. The IG found that the Justice Department classified 762 of the detainees as "September 11 detainees." The IG concluded that none of these detainees were charged with terrorist-related offenses, and that the decision to detain them was "extremely attenuated" from the 9/11 investigation. The IG concluded that the Justice Department's designation of detainees of interest to the 9/11 investigation was "indiscriminate and haphazard," and did not adequately distinguish between terrorism suspects and other immigration detainees.

The IG also found detainees were subjected to harsh conditions of confinement, including cells that were illuminated 24 hours per day, and confinement to their cells for all but one hour per day. Disturbingly, the IG also found "a pattern of physical and verbal abuse by some correctional officers at the MDC [Metropolitan Detention Center in Brooklyn, New York] against some September 11 detainees, particularly during the first months after the attacks."

I'm not suggesting that the government should never use immigration charges to detain a suspected terrorist, but the broad brush of terrorism should not be applied to every out-of-status immigrant who happens to be Arab or Muslim. Our immigration system is fundamentally broken. Comprehensive immigration reform is required to address this problem. We should not confuse the problems with our immigration system with our efforts to combat terrorism. Detaining large numbers of undocumented Arab and Muslim immigrants will not aid our efforts to combat terrorism, and might actually harm them. . . .

Damaging Interviews

The Justice Department also launched the "Interview Project," to interview thousands of Arabs and Muslims, including U.S. citizens. The Arab American Institute found that these interviews created fear and suspicion in the community, especially among recent immigrants, and damaged our efforts to build bridges between the community and law enforcement.

Like other DOJ programs that cast a wide net, the interviews created a public impression that federal law enforcement views our entire community with suspicion, which, in some cases, fostered discrimination. For example, we received reports of instances where the FBI visited individuals at their workplace, and then these individuals were subsequently demoted or terminated by their employers.

FBI officials with whom I have spoken also questioned the project's usefulness as a law enforcement and counterterrorism program. They told me it involved a significant investment of manpower, produced little useful information, and damaged their community outreach efforts.

The General Accounting Office [GAO] reviewed the Interview Project and concluded:

> How and to what extent the interview project—
> including investigative leads and increased presence of law enforcement in communities—helped
> the government combat terrorism is hard to measure . . . More than half of the law enforcement officers that [the GAO] interviewed raised concerns
> about the quality of the questions or the value of
> the responses.

According to the GAO, "Attorneys and advocates told us that interviewed aliens told them that they felt they were being singled out and investigated because of their ethnicity or religious beliefs." The GAO also concluded that many of those interviewed "did not feel the interviews were truly voluntary," and feared "repercussions" if they declined to be interviewed.

The Toll of Civil Liberties Abuses

I am concerned about these and other government efforts that infringe upon civil liberties for several reasons. First, it is wrong to single out innocent people based on their ethnicity or religion. This runs contrary to the uniquely American ideal of equal protection under the law.

By casting such a wide net, these efforts squander precious law enforcement resources and alienate communities whose cooperation law enforcement needs. They run counter to basic principles of community policing, which reject the use of racial and ethnic profiles and focus on building trust and respect by working cooperatively with community members.

> The Justice Department's efforts are taking a toll in the Arab American community.

According to polls conducted by the Arab American Institute and Zogby International, the Justice Department's efforts are taking a toll in the Arab American community. Immediately after 9/11 Arab Americans were heartened by President Bush's strong display of support for the community. In October 2001, 90% said that they were reassured by the President's support, while only six percent were not reassured. By May 2002, those who felt reassured dropped to 54% as opposed to 35% who were not. In a July 2003 poll, the ratio dropped even further, with only 49% now saying that they feel assured by Bush's support for the community while 38% say that they are not assured. Thirty percent of Arab Americans report having experienced some form of discrimination, and 60% say they are now concerned about the long-term impact of discrimination against Arab Americans.

Civil liberties abuses against Arabs and Muslims have been well-publicized in the Arab world, and there is a growing perception that Arab immigrants and visitors are not welcome in the United States. As a result, America is less popular, and it is more politically difficult for our Arab allies to cooperate with our counterterrorism efforts. . . .

Abuses Harm American Credibility

Due to a variety of factors, including fear of discrimination, many fewer Arabs come to the U.S. for medical treatment, tourism, study, or business. In the past, Arab visitors to the U.S. have had a chance to observe first-hand the unique nature of American democracy and freedom and have returned to the Arab world as ambassadors for our values.

In his address on November 6 [2003], President Bush rightly linked the spread of democracy to the war on terrorism. Unfortunately, civil liberties abuses against Arabs and Muslims in the U.S. have undermined our openness and have harmed our ability to advocate credibly for democratic reforms in the Middle East. In fact, some Arab governments now point to American practices to justify their own human rights abuses. As President Bush suggested, and as we have learned so painfully, anti-democratic practices and human rights abuses promote instability and create the conditions that breed terrorism. Democratic reformers and human rights activists used to look to the U.S. as an exemplar, the city on a hill. Now they are dismissed by their countrymen when they point to the American experience.

Once we set a high standard for the world, now we have lowered the bar. The damage to our image, to the values we have sought to project, and to our ability to deal more effectively with root causes of terror have been profound.

7

American Muslims Do Not Experience Discrimination

Daniel Pipes

Daniel Pipes is the director of the Middle East Forum and the author of numerous articles and books on Islam, including Militant Islam Reaches America, *from which the following viewpoint was excerpted.*

Bias toward American Muslims is not a significant problem. Despite the lack of serious discrimination toward Muslims, the American media, school system, and employers go out of their way to rectify the most minor of offenses. Drastic actions, such as the firings of employees who offend their Muslim colleagues, indicate how powerful this group has become. While many American Muslims realize that they are treated well by U.S. institutions and fellow citizens, Muslim organizations continue to claim that American Muslims are discriminated against. By promoting victimization and fueling grievances, these organizations convince Muslims to support them financially.

Muslims are undoubtedly right when they say that Islam suffers from a poor reputation in the United States. But they cannot complain about receptivity to their complaints. Public figures who make statements perceived as inimical to Islam by Muslim groups usually apologize right away. Two days after Senator Joseph Biden, Jr. (Democrat of Delaware), worried on television that bombing Iraq might "embolden Islam to become more aggressive with the United States," he contradicted his words: "Islam is one of the world's great religions. It stands for peace, tolerance, and justice and it is responsible for many enlightening advances in human thought and practice over the centuries."

Speedy Retractions

When the media offends Muslims or makes a factual mistake, an apology or retraction follows with (uncharacteristic) speed. Jay Leno of NBC's *Tonight Show* apologized for a seemingly inoffensive comedy sketch about an imaginary amusement park in Iran and promised to be "more diligent in the future." Martin Goldsmith, host of National Public Radio's *Performance Today*, related a legend about the Prophet Muhammad relying on special coffee to "make love to forty women in one night" over forty nights. He soon offered "sincere apologies" for giving offense and thanked his listeners for making their concerns known. After Paul Harvey, said to be the most listened to radio broadcaster in America, called Islam a "fraudulent religion," he quickly dubbed this an "unintentional slur" and duly apologized on air for having "understandably offended" Muslims.

Jewish media do likewise. The *Jewish Journal* in Miami published a letter to the editor stating that "Muslims are killing non-Muslims worldwide. Israel is beset by these animals on all sides with no peace possible. . . . Adherents of Islam are indeed insane. There will never be peace on earth as long as they exist." The editors then apologized to "our Islam brothers" for comments that "went beyond the limits of civilized discourse."

> *"The Internet follows . . . special rules for Muslims, who are protected from the sort of things routinely said about blacks or Jews."*

Book publishers do more; they actually recall books, at considerable expense to themselves. Simon & Schuster withdrew a children's book, *Great Lives: World Religions* by William Jay Jacobs, when made aware of its treatment of the Prophet Muhammad ("He took pleasure in seeing the heads of his enemies torn from their bodies by the swords of his soldiers").

Books are also recalled when they contain nothing particularly egregious, only mistakes. That was the case with *Muslim Holidays* by Faith Winchester; the publisher, Capstone Press, called the book back because it showed pictures of Muhammad, transliterated a holiday in a nonstandard way, and repeated some odd folk tales.

The Internet follows these same special rules for Muslims, who are protected from the sort of things routinely said about blacks or Jews. AT&T WorldNet Service removed a site that defamed the Prophet Muhammad as a "rapist" and found him worse than Adolf Hitler. GeoCities took down a Web site that called Islam "a threat to the whole world" and profaned the Prophet ("Mohammed The Playboy" and "Prophet Mohammed's Libido Exposed!"). America Online closed down a site that published pseudo-Qur'anic verses, on the grounds that it was "clearly designed to be hurtful and defamatory." This is not prejudice but kid-glove treatment.

Widespread Hypersensitivity

The military is no less sensitive. When U.S. forces bombed Iraqi targets in late 1998, sailors on the USS *Enterprise* engaged in the time-hallowed practice of scribbling aggressive graffiti on a bomb; the Associated Press ran a picture showing an inscription: "Here's a Ramadan present from Chad Rickenberg." When a Muslim group protested this "bigoted sentiment," the Pentagon spokesman expressed distress at what it called "thoughtless graffiti" and dismissed the episode as "a rare exception that does not reflect American policy or values."

As one might expect, schools are hypersensitive. A professor at Southern Connecticut State University allegedly gave an anti-Islamic tract to a student; the university responded by instituting educational seminars on Islam. An assistant professor at Southeast Oklahoma State University, a convert to Islam, complained that colleagues continued to use his former name; in response, a representative of Oklahoma's coordinating board for higher education communicated his concerns "to the appropriate officials . . . to take appropriate action." More drastic action is not uncommon. A high school teacher in Rochester, Minnesota, was reassigned for expressing dislike of Muslim modesty practices; and a school official warned that "One misstep and she's gone." A New Jersey professor who said "Goddamn Muslims" in front of a class was reportedly out of a job.

Advertisements that take the faith lightly are withdrawn with alacrity. Total Sports, Inc., canceled an ad showing a group of Muslims "praying" to a basketball. Burger King pulled an ad in which a character bearing a Muslim name ("Rasheed") praises the restaurant chain's bacon-laden Whopper sandwich. The Colorado Lottery pulled radio advertisements that began: "You've heard the old expression about the mountain coming to Mohammed?" on the grounds that Islam forbids gambling. The *Los Angeles Times* dropped its ad campaign contrasting two types of readers—bikini-clad and chador-clad—because Muslims objected. Many other companies—including Anheuser-Busch, DoubleTree Hotels, MasterCard International, Miller Brewing Company, Seagrams, and Timeslips Corporation—also withdrew ads after hearing Muslim complaints.

> *American Muslims . . . are benefiting from the government readiness to dictate workplace rules.*

The use of Arabic for decorative purposes often arouses Muslim objections, due to its sacral associations, and corporations respond quickly. Warehouse One withdrew a women's shirt with Arabic script from the Qur'an on the front and the sleeves. Liz Claiborne discontinued the use of Arabic lettering from the Qur'an on its clothes and issued an abject apology ("We are profoundly sorry that any of our products reflected insensitivity toward the Muslim faith, as this was certainly never our intent"). The willingness not to offend Muslim sensibility reached a climax when CAIR (Council on American-Islamic Relations) contended that the logo on a Nike basketball shoe could "be interpreted" as the word "Allah" (God) in Arabic script. Though Nike denied any such intent (the logo was to look like flames, not Arabic letters), the threat of a worldwide boycott by Muslims prompted Nike to withdraw the shoe, investigate the incident, introduce changes in its design shop, learn about Islamic designs, and produce educational CDs and videos about Islam. Nor was that all; Nike also agreed to sponsor events in the Muslim community, donate Nike products to Islamic charitable groups, and pay for sports facilities at several Islamic schools (the first payment was $50,000 for the Dar Al-

Hijrah Islamic Center in northern Virginia).

Employees with grievances sometimes make out well in court. Lule Said, a Somali immigrant, was working in 1991 as a guard for Northeast Security of Brookline, Massachusetts, when a co-worker complained about his origins and faith, announced that he hated Muslims, wiped his feet on Said's prayer rug and kicked it aside, then threatened him. Said complained to his supervisor but was told to stop praying or he would lose his job. The Massachusetts Commission Against Discrimination awarded Said $300,000 (about a decade worth's of his salary) for these tribulations and chewed out Northeast Security: "This case uniquely demonstrates . . . the debilitating impact discrimination has on an individual's well-being." Ahmad Abu-Aziz, an immigrant from Jordan, claimed that from the start of his employment for United Air Lines in California in 1994, he faced discrimination—being compared to a terrorist, his name ridiculed, derogatory comments about his religion and national origin, unfair work assignments. When Abu-Aziz complained to his supervisor, he was ignored, then terminated for supposed misconduct. He went to court and a jury awarded him $2.9 million in damages, a sum sustained by appellate court.

In other words, just as American Muslims have benefited from multiculturalism, so they are benefiting from the government readiness to dictate workplace rules.

American Muslims Are Treated Well

American Muslims fully recognize their fortunate circumstances. A mid-1980s survey found that "No Muslim interviewed reported that he or she had ever experienced any personal harassment in the workplace or knew of any experienced by a friend or associate as a result of being either Muslim or foreign-born. Nor did any of those interviewed report any problems in buying or renting homes or apartments as a result of perceived prejudice." An early 1990s study into Muslim youth found that all the women interviewed "denied they were oppressed in any way in the United States." In 2000, an AMC [American Muslim Council] poll found 66.1 percent of Muslims agreeing with the assertion that "U.S. society currently shows a respect towards the Muslim faith."

Individual Muslims concur. Fereydun Hoveyda, a former Iranian official now living in New York, finds that in the United States "there is no animosity at all to Islam. Jeffrey Lang, the

58

Christian-born professor of mathematics, writes of his conversion to Islam: "I do not believe it has greatly affected my career." "Our life in this county has been terrific and we love it," an immigrant to Virginia named Hisham Elbasha tells *The Washington Post*. Muslims also note that bias is diminishing; in 1999 a young Muslim in Washington said he witnessed "increased tolerance observing the month of Ramadan this year."

> **" What bias against Muslims does exist is contained, illegal, and of relatively little import. "**

Even those same Muslim organizations that complain about discrimination and "Islamophobia" sometimes admit that things are going well. Ibrahim Hooper of CAIR, one of the most vocal supporters of this position, acknowledges that "Domestic policy towards the Muslim community is quite good." His boss, Nihad Awad, makes a similar point, that "here anti-Muslim feelings have no roots, unlike Europe." Institutionally, CAIR finds that things are better in the United States than in some Muslim countries: "Muslims in America," it has said, "take for granted rights routinely denied to their co-religionists in Turkey." Khaled Saffuri of the Islamic Institute goes further, conceding that in the United States, "there is relatively speaking a better degree of freedom compared to many Muslim countries." It all sounds very good indeed.

Eagerness to Oblige Muslims

All this is not to deny that some bias against Muslims does exist. But no immigrant group or non-Protestant religion is wholly free of this. Buddhists and Hindus, adherents of religions yet more alien to most Americans, also face prejudices and are subjected to ridicule. Their temples are on occasion vandalized with swastikas smeared on temple walls, with one attack specifically timed to take place on the anniversary of *Kristallnacht*, the Nazi rampage against Jews in 1938. Buddhists and Hindus do not receive the favorable media treatment accorded Islam. Yet they hardly complain, much less do they have a protest industry.

Further, what bias against Muslims does exist is contained, illegal, and of relatively little import. Linda S. Walbridge, an anthropologist who immersed herself in an American Muslim community, offers a useful comparison with anti-Catholic sentiment: the latter "has not disappeared from America, but it is at a low enough level that it certainly does not hinder Catholics from participating in all spheres of activity. There is no reason to think that Muslims . . . will experience anything much different." Adjustment is needed, to be sure, to accommodate a new and still alien faith: employers have to learn about beards, headscarves, prayers, and fasts; advertisers will take a while to understand Muslim sensitivities. Nonetheless, the record shows an impressive flexibility on the part of American institutions, public and private, to acknowledge Islam and oblige Muslims. To help the process along, Muslims have considerable sway over the media and are in the process of building an impressive lobbying organization.

If one were to speculate about the reasons for this happy circumstance, two explanations spring to mind. One is American openness to the immigrant and the exotic, combined with a historic disposition to offer a level playing field to all. The other is a genuine multiculturalism—not the specious doctrine of racial and ethnic "diversity" imposed so successfully on American institutions but a sincere willingness to accept and learn from other civilizations. Other factors play a part as well, including the growth of the regulatory arm of government and especially its readiness to dictate workplace rules. American Muslims have been quick to avail themselves of these benefits, as is, of course, their right.

It is also the right of CAIR, AMC, and the Muslim Public Affairs Council to devote their resources to promoting the idea of Muslim victimization. They do so for the same reasons that some other ethnic and religious defense groups do—to pay the bills and fuel the grievances they hope to ride. But the reality is stubbornly otherwise: far from being victimized, the Muslim American community is robust and advancing steadily. For non-Muslim Americans, the lesson should be clear: even as they continue to welcome active Muslim participation in American life, there is no reason to fall for, let alone to endorse, spurious charges of "discrimination and harassment."

8

The Rights of Muslim American Women Are Violated by Muslim Men

Barbara J. Stock

Barbara J. Stock is a registered nurse and contributor to ChronWatch, a Web site that features conservative news and commentary.

Troubling changes are occurring in the lives of Muslim American women. While these women have long considered themselves equal to men, the rising influence of Arab Muslim immigrants in the U.S. Muslim community is placing American women at risk. Arab Muslim men have a negative influence on their U.S.-born counterparts and refuse to follow American laws. As a result Muslim American women are being segregated from men in mosques and are shunned by fellow Muslims if they report spousal abuse. In general, the influence of Arab Muslim men is threatening women's equality. Muslim American women must fight back, which may entail choosing between freedom and Islam.

As I read e-mail messages that I have received in response to my columns about Islam, I began to realize that 99.9% of the responses were from men. Thinking back, I remember receiving only three messages from Muslim women.

Barbara J. Stock, "The Plight of Muslim Women," *Chronwatch News & Editorial*, January 22, 2005. Copyright © 2005 by Barbara J. Stock. Reproduced by permission.

Three Perspectives

One was a young woman from California who desperately wanted to get out the word that not all Muslims were terrorists. Of course, being an American Muslim, her Muslim acquaintances were probably not terrorists. I told her that she could write a column or whatever she wished and I would post it on my website.

This brave, young woman excitedly told me she would love to post a column but would have to seek permission from her Imam [religious leader].

I never heard from her again.

Another respondent was an obviously wealthy, educated woman who admitted that she lived in a country that was a democracy. She was safe and protected—by the laws of the land and her money. She wholeheartedly supported the terrorists. This woman, in her arrogance, ignored the plight of her fellow female Muslims around the world. Her life was good and that was all she cared about.

> *Many women feel that the influx of Arab Muslim men to America is having a bad influence on American Muslim men.*

The third respondent was a young woman from Saudi Arabia who freely admitted that much of what I said was true. She also insisted that life in the kingdom was not so bad for women anymore. Apparently she has already forgotten the 15 young girls forced to burn to death by the Islamic police behind a locked gate because they sinned by not covering their heads in public. I have been told that there was outrage from the Saudi people over this terrible act, which is good, but the men responsible were never punished for outright murder. In fact, excuses were made for them by a Royal Family which was apparently afraid to push the radical element too far.

This young Saudi lady was saddened that Islam has been given such a bad name by a "few." Yes, there were many in her country that hated America, but not all. Well, that's comforting for Americans. In this case, because her life "wasn't so bad," this young woman seemed oblivious to the treatment of Muslim women in strict Islamic states. She also seemed blissfully unaware that she is only a heartbeat away from the same fate. When I pointed out the treatment of women in strict Islamic states, she ceased communication.

Disturbing Changes

I began to wonder what the women of Islam were thinking here in the United States and how they are being treated. There was a time when life for Muslim women in America was very good. They lived as other American women lived. For some, the lucky ones, it remains good. There have been ominous changes, however, and American Muslim women find these changes very disturbing.

American Muslim women feel that they interpret the Quran correctly. They feel that men and women are equal and a marriage is a partnership, just as in any society. Pre-Mohammed, Arab women were quite successful. They owned businesses, could obtain divorces from abusive or lazy men, inherit wealth, own land, and were educated. Mohammed and Islam changed all that. Where in the Quran American Muslim women are reading about the equality of the sexes is a mystery to me. The passages I have read speak only of the superiority of men and the weakness of women.

Strict Islamics bolster their own power by considering women physically, mentally, and intellectually inferior to men. When Ayatollah Ruhollah Khomeini succeeded in his Islamic revolution in Iran, one of his first edicts to Muslim men was, "Your wife, who is your possession, is in fact, your slave." Women in Iran have lived in terror for years. In the mid-1980's, Khomeini realized he needed more bodies to fight Iraq, women were suddenly elevated—at least high enough to become cannon fodder.

Poor Treatment Throughout the World

Life for Iranian women became slightly better after Khomeini's death. But [in 2004] humanitarian groups fought to save the life of a 13 year old girl sentenced to be stoned to death because her brother had raped her. Without the required three male witnesses to the act, the women who are raped are the ones that are punished as harlots. Such is life in Iran for Muslim women.

Everyone should be familiar with how women were treated by the Taliban in Afghanistan. They were beaten if the wind blew their skirt and an ankle became visible and publicly executed in soccer stadiums for such crimes as leaving their home without a male family member's permission. Women had no value in that barbaric Islamic state. A man probably would not treat his cow as he treated his wife or daughter.

> **❝** *American Muslim women, who were always allowed to go to mosque and pray with the men, are now finding themselves shunted to separate rooms.* **❞**

Even in Western countries, honor killings happen almost on a daily basis. Any Muslim woman who marries without permission, even to a Muslim man, is subject to execution by her father, brothers, uncles, or any male family member who feels that he was slighted. Young girls that are raped are often killed on the spot by enraged fathers or brothers who feel that it was the woman's fault and these unfortunate girls are now "soiled" and a disgrace to the family. Arab Muslims who immigrate to Western countries tend to cluster in neighborhoods and isolate themselves, bringing their Arab Islamic traditions with them. Men who rape are rarely punished. The Islamic community protects those committing honor killings.

Another horrific tradition inflicted on Muslim girls is female circumcision. This is done without any anesthesia and is for the sole reason of robbing the woman of any pleasure from sex. This is an honor reserved for men only. Surely women will sin if they receive any pleasure from the sex act. Men, however, will not.

A Loss of Equality for Muslim Women

So how are American Muslim women faring these days? The American Muslim websites I read had mixed views. Many women feel that the influx of Arab Muslim men to America is having a bad influence on American Muslim men. They are ridiculing them for allowing their women to work, go to college, and "show their bodies." They are convincing many American Muslim men that American life is un-Islamic.

These Arab immigrants are also refusing to follow the American law of only having one wife. They take more wives and marry them only under the laws of Islam. When they become bored with them, they just turn them out on the streets with their children. Because they were never legally married in the eyes of American law, these women have no legal recourse.

American Muslim women, who were always allowed to go to mosque and pray with the men, are now finding themselves shunted to separate rooms where the words of the Imam may or may not be piped in via loudspeaker. Only men are allowed in the main part of the mosque. Women, once equals, are now finding themselves on the outside looking in, literally. They don't like it.

If a wife is beaten by her husband and dares to report it to the police, she is shunned by her fellow Muslims. Taking such problems to outsiders is considered un-Islamic but Islamic leaders have no pity for women beaten by cruel husbands or fathers. Obviously, they had done something to deserve it. Battered wives have no recourse within Islamic law.

A Difficult Choice

This seems to be a pattern of Islam. Native Muslims, peaceful and friendly with their neighbors sometimes for hundreds of years, are infiltrated by Arab Muslims who quickly begin to exert their influence and seize power. Soon, life is not good for the Muslim woman.

American Muslim women have more opportunity to fight back because the law of the land is on their side. However, to benefit from this protection, many must often make the choice—freedom or Islam. It is a difficult decision for them to make. Even here in America, the fear of punishment is ever-present. Fear of isolation and loss of family support weighs heavily on these battered women. The good news is American Muslim women are fighting back. I wish them luck.

One has to wonder if the words "Islam" and "freedom" can even be used together. Those two words seem diametrically opposed to each other. There is no Islamic country in the world that is free. I have been repeatedly told that Islam is peaceful. But there is no peace or freedom under Islamic rule anywhere in the world.

9

African American Muslims Are Treated Like Second-Class Citizens

Michelle Cottle

Michelle Cottle is a senior editor for the New Republic.

Islam has been practiced by African Americans for several centuries. Despite this lengthy history, African American Muslims often feel that their experiences and perspectives are ignored by immigrant Muslims, who treat their African American counterparts like second-class citizens. Muslims from other countries present themselves as the spokespeople for their religion even though African Americans have a superior understanding of America. Unfortunately, when African American leaders have had the opportunity to speak about Islam, they have often chosen to use the opportunity to condemn America, which they feel is racist.

You didn't need to go trick-or-treating on Halloween [2001] to get a good scare. All you had to do was flip on C-span2 any time between 7 and 11 o'clock and watch the "New Black Panther Party and Muslims for Truth and Justice Town Hall Meeting" at the National Press Club in Washington. Moderated by Panther Amir Muhammad, the event featured a parade of exceedingly angry imams [spiritual leaders], activists, and audience members melding black-power salutes and Koranic quotations with loud denunciations of the United States as "the Great Satan." Beefy Panthers in military-style garb formed a menacing backdrop for prayer leaders peddling conspiracy theories—in particular, the U.S. government and media's cover up of Israel's role in every terrorist episode from the 1998 American Embassy bombings to the September 11 [2001] hijackings. Uncle Sam, charged Amir Muhammad, "is the number-one oppressor in the history of the planet Earth, the number-one murderer on the planet Earth, and the number-one spreader of terror on the planet Earth."

Flash forward two days to Friday services at Masjid Muhammad in Northwest D.C. Inside the prayer hall, some 150 worshipers sit beneath whirring fans, listening to visiting Imam Abdul Malik Mohammed denounce the C-span event. "Do you want me to believe that the environment that guarantees me protection to pray five times a day and that ordains itself, its credibility, under God's trust—you want me to suspect it? To feel bad about it?" he bellows. "Go to hell!" The imam not only defends the United States, he suggests it is the Middle East where something has gone badly wrong with Islam. "[W]hile the Muslim World has had the Koran and they have recited the Koran and the Koran has dwelled in their hearts . . . I contend that, in view of circumstances that we have witnessed for many years, Mohammed the Prophet is not known to them." Chiding listeners to stop deferring to foreign-born Muslims just because "they step before you and they're wearing robes and turbans and it makes you think they're back there with Mohammed the Prophet," he argues that Old World Muslims have been mere "warm-up speakers" for African Americans. "God is correcting [misconceptions of] Islam in the world," he says, "and he is not correcting it in the East! He is correcting it in the West!"

Difficult to Talk About Islam

In fact, during these troubled times, African American Muslims should be well positioned to do much "correcting" of American misperceptions about Islam, not to mention Muslim misperceptions of the United States. African American Muslims are, after all, living proof that Islam has deep roots on these shores. That it need not speak with a foreign accent. That it is no more alien, or hostile, than the streets of Harlem, Chicago, or East St. Louis, where it thrives.

But then, that is precisely the problem. The people who

might best speak to the Muslim world about the United States are themselves often deeply conflicted Americans. For every imam like Abdul Malik Mohammed, who promotes a distinctly American Islam, free from the hatreds of the Middle East, there is an Amir Muhammed, whose Islam represents a direct rejection of American culture, a righteous banner under which African Americans must rally against their historical oppressors.

But if it's difficult for black Muslims to speak to the Islamic world as proud Americans, it's often just as difficult for them to speak to Americans about Islam. For most Americans, Muslim means Arab. And black leaders complain that, for too long, immigrant Muslims have set themselves up as the sole gatekeepers of the faith. As a result, instead of now serving as ambassadors for their religion or for their country, many African American Muslims feel trapped in the center of a storm, unable to make themselves heard, and unsure, perhaps, of even what they want to say.

> *It's often . . . difficult for [black Muslims] to speak to Americans about Islam.*

It's no secret that "the black community has its own beef with the white community," notes Aminah McCloud, an associate professor of Religious Studies at DePaul University in Chicago. Indeed, the very roots of Islam among African Americans are tangled up in the fight against white racism. Though Islam first arrived here in the hull of slave ships, it didn't catch fire until the 1950s and 1960s, with the rise of the Nation of Islam under the late Elijah Mohammed and Malcolm X. Initially bearing little resemblance to orthodox Islam, the Nation peddled a black nationalist ideology that was more about toppling white power than serving Allah. Today, though most African American Muslims practice a more traditional Islam, traces of racial struggle remain, both in sermons and in the way congregants interpret Islam's message.

All of which makes it hard for African American Muslims to tell their brethren overseas that the United States does not hate their faith. Nationwide, polls show that black Americans are more critical than whites of the U.S. war on terror, and in certain circles suspicion runs high that the government is using

September 11 as an excuse to wage war on Islam. "We know, as only people who have lived subserviently among Caucasians can, that the white men who run the country . . . are lying," says McCloud's husband, Frederick Thaufeer al-Deen, formerly an imam with the federal prison system. This so-called war on terror is just the government's latest attempt to justify unjust foreign policy decisions ranging from the support of Palestinian oppression to the presence of U.S. troops in Saudi Arabia, he says. "We're trying to do something over there that is wrong."

Empathy for Osama bin Laden

In this worldview, [Islamic terrorist] Osama bin Laden is more scapegoat than villain. The always controversial Louis Farrakhan made waves recently with his demand for the United States to produce evidence of bin Laden's guilt—a call echoed more quietly by many in the black community. Ghayth Nut Kashif, imam of the Masjidush-Shura in Southeast Washington, [D.C.,] does not say explicitly whether he believes bin Laden to be innocent, but compares the U.S. hunt for the Saudi exile to "the Klan-type activities" of the 1930s and 1940s. "Whenever something happened to a white girl or white woman," he recalls, "people would grab the first black man who was about the right height and age." Now he and others insist that bin Laden is being similarly targeted. "When [Bush] said he wanted [bin Laden] dead or alive," a local pastor told *The Washington Post*, "he was calling out the posse, and black people know the posse. They come by and get you in the middle of the night and kill you without due process." Some go even further. "For the record, I love Osama bin Laden," says al-Deen. "I don't excuse any tactic he had to use by being a guerrilla-warfare fighter, but I understand."

One voice notably absent from the public arena has been W. Deen Mohammed, son of the late Elijah Mohammed and head of the Muslim American Society, the nation's largest organization of African American Muslims. In 1975 it was W. Deen who rejected the racialist ideology of the Nation of Islam and led the group's members into orthodox Sunnism (opening a schism with black-power advocates like Farrakhan that has only begun to heal in the past year or so). W. Deen is arguably the most authoritative voice for black Muslims. But since issuing a brief condemnation of the September 11 attacks and a plea for Muslims to "stay calm and remain in our good sense," the imam has remained largely silent, leaving a chorus of others to fill the void. Which is a pity. Because if African Americans don't reject the loud voices spewing hate-filled messages, Imam Abdul Malik Mohammed (a devotee of W. Deen) warned the folks at Masjid Muhammad, the radicals will taint the entire community. "Persons will watch this and associate that kind of thinking with us," he said. Americans will see all of this "ugly ranting and raving, this irresponsible language," and think of all Muslims, "This is what they feel in their hearts."

> *The immigrant community itself at times treats African Americans as second-class Muslims.*

But if many African American Muslims reject the role of American ambassadors to their coreligionists, they also face obstacles in serving as interpreters of Islam for a U.S. audience. "When folks want to know about Islam, they have always gone to the immigrant community," gripes McCloud. It's telling, she says, that after September 11, "who came to the White House to represent Islam? The immigrant community. The African American community felt very dismayed." Even Oprah Winfrey has been accused of bias: Kashif's wife, Hafeeza, says she was dismayed one afternoon to see "all these Muslims on—and not one was African American."

Second-Class Treatment

In part, this is because when most Americans think of American Muslims, they think of immigrants. But it's also because the immigrant community itself at times treats African Americans as second-class Muslims. "I used to be around a lot of Eastern Muslims," says Muhammad Abdul Rahman, a member of Masjidush-Shura. "They would come over here and treat us like we were babes in Islam. They thought they should be our leaders just because they could speak Arabic. They would come into [our] masjids and try to be our teachers." September 11, he says, "is bringing all this stuff back up."

The divide is partly cultural and economic. McCloud notes, "We have in the African American community a host of imams who are men who work full-time jobs. . . . They don't have the luxury of being paid to be just an imam." Al-Deen, expressing the views of many he counseled over the years, puts it more bluntly: "They have the money and we don't. It's a sour-grapes kind of thing." And, he says, Muslim immigrants have traditionally failed to reach out to African Americans: "They come over with their money and their degrees and with an insular view of Islam. . . . They hide in their jobs and their little communities."

For a people long considered second-class citizens within their own country, being treated like second-class citizens within their own religion is a sore point—particularly now, when Islam's role in America is a topic of unprecedented public debate. "Our role in America is critical," says Imam Kashif. "Immigrant Muslims to a great extent don't know the terrain. They don't understand the European mind—the American authorities' mind. We do." It's a nice thought. Until you realize that what many in Kashif's community "understand" about the American mind is that it insists on viewing Osama bin Laden as guilty, when in truth he's just another innocent victim.

10
Islam Is Gaining Popularity Among Hispanic Americans

Lisa Viscidi

Lisa Viscidi is a legal researcher and a former staff member of Washington Report on Middle East Affairs.

A growing number of American Latinos are becoming Muslims. Many of these Muslims are former Catholics who converted to Islam because they were uncomfortable with the hierarchy and practices of Catholicism. In addition, Islam appeals to Hispanic Americans because Islam has had a lengthy historical and cultural connection with Spain. The key Muslim beliefs of racial equality and unity further attract the often-struggling Latinos, who find in Islam emotional and practical support.

On Jan. 21, 2003, the United States Census Bureau officially named the nation's 37 million Latinos the country's largest minority population—outnumbering African Americans by 0.3 percent. This demographic shift, coupled with Islam's status as the fastest growing religion in America, has contributed to the significant growth of a newly emerging demographic: Latino Muslims.

Lacking an organized network, and with their cultural presence in this country a relatively recent one, Latino Muslims are not as visible as other U.S. minority groups. Nevertheless, their existence is becoming evident around the country. The Latino Muslim presence is particularly prominent in New York, Southern California and Chicago—places where both Hispanics and Muslims reside in great numbers. These cities boast Latino mosques and organizations exclusively directed toward the Latino Muslim community. The Islamic Society of North America's annual conference on Latino Muslims, and the recently established Latino Coordinating Committee attest to the growing importance of this group in American Muslim society.

> *Latinos convert to Islam for a variety of reasons, including disenchantment with the practices of Catholicism and the church establishment.*

Although the exact number of Latino Muslims is difficult to determine, estimates range from 25,000 to 60,000. This includes second- or third-generation Hispanic Americans as well as recent immigrants.

Comparing Islam and Catholicism

While some Latinos were reared Muslim, many have converted from Catholicism. Latinos convert to Islam for a variety of reasons, including disenchantment with the practices of Catholicism and the church establishment. These Latinos are lured by Islam's simplicity and the Muslim's independence of a mediating clergy in his or her relationship with God. According to Juan Galvan, vice president of the Latino American Dawah Organization, "Most Hispanic converts were Catholic. Many Hispanics had difficulty with the church, believing in original sin, and in the Holy Trinity. Islam solves the problems many Hispanics have with the Catholic Church. For example, in Islam there is no priest-pope hierarchy. Everyone who prays before God is equal. Many Latino converts feel Islam gives them a closer relationship to God." Other Latinos find the church's historical associations objectionable. Rather than viewing Catholicism as the native religion of their culture, they protest that Catholicism was originally forced on their indigenous ancestors by Europeans. The church's past involvement in Latin America and the suffering caused by colonization have tarnished its image for many Latinos. Notes Dr. Fathi Osman, resident scholar at the

Omar Foundation, an Islamic cultural and educational center, "In their own countries Hispanics did not see the church supporting the rights of the poor. Rather it sided with the rich and the influential. It can be difficult to make a distinction between the church or clergy and the religion itself."

Islam, on the other hand, offers many Latinos more appealing historical ties. Citing a heritage that dates back to Spain's classical Islamic period, many Latino Muslims claim that conversion to Islam represents a return to their true cultural traditions.

Indeed, beginning in 711 A.D. with the Muslim general Tariq ibn Ziad's conquest of the Spanish Peninsula, the Muslim Moors ruled Spain for nearly eight centuries. During that period, Islamic influence penetrated many facets of life, including music, architecture and literature. This influence was abetted by Islam's religious tolerance, which enabled Christians, Jews and Muslims to coexist relatively peacefully. Conversion to Islam was encouraged but not forced. With the fall of the last Muslim stronghold in 1492 and the ensuing Inquisition, however, Muslims as well as Jews were forced to convert to Christianity or be exiled.

As the Inquisition raged in Spain, the Conquistadores began trafficking Muslim slaves from Africa to the New World, and Islam thus traveled to Latin America. The religion spread throughout the continent, fueled in the mid–19th century by a massive migration of Muslim Arabs.

A Historical Connection

Many Latinos who convert to Islam believe they are reclaiming their lost Muslim and African heritage—which they view more positively than the legacy of Catholicism. Many Spanish intellectuals once disputed the extent of Moorish influence on Hispanic culture, but Latino Muslims who claim African and Islamic roots question the view of Western society's origins as exclusively European. They point to the African/Islamic influence evident in Spanish literature, music and thought. Thousands of Spanish words, for example, are derived from Arabic. Ibrahim Gonzalez, a Muslim convert whose parents moved to New York City from Puerto Rico, claims that "in Latino culture, especially language, there are lots of 'Arabisms.'" As Islam spread throughout Latin America, Gonzalez believes, it helped to shape Latino culture.

Islam's appeal for Latinos is not only historical, however.

Just as many Latino Muslims believe that Christianity was once an elitist religion that failed to protect their indigenous ancestors, many Latinos today feel that the church does not adequately defend the Latino-American struggle for equality. Alienation from Christian American society, along with poor social and economic conditions, may divert Latinos from Christianity—the religion of the establishment that, they believe, ignores their needs. According to the Omar Foundation's Osman, as a minority, Latinos are not understood or supported by the U.S. church, which, he says, continues to side with the elite. In Osman's view, the Catholic Church advocates equality and justice in theory, but does not implement them in practice. "Most Latinos are poor and feel oppressed," he contends. "They don't get justice in their original countries or in the U.S. They want a religion that cares about those who are oppressed."

> *For impoverished Latinos and African Americans living in inner cities, Islam provides material as well as spiritual support.*

In Islam many Latinos find a community more sympathetic to their plight. Muslims, who are also a minority in the U.S., identify more closely with the Latino struggle for justice and equality. Estranged from mainstream Christian America, Latinos can identify with and take pride in the Muslim community and in Islam's past.

Gonzalez, a co-founder of the Latino Muslim organization Alianza Islamica, says he "grew up in a revolutionary environment. East Harlem was a center for political activism and the struggle for human rights of people of all colors. We had fervor to continue the struggle but no place to go. We were disenfranchised. We sought other outlets and came upon Islam. We became serious young men seeking to elevate ourselves within our society. We got this from Islam."

Islam Appeals to Minorities

Perhaps Islam's doctrine of racial equality and unity accounts for part of its appeal to minority groups. Substantial numbers of African Americans also have converted to Islam in recent decades. The religion unifies various American minorities whose social and economic circumstances often are similar. Gonzalez describes Islam as "a universal faith where people of all walks of life pray together. Religion unifies culture and enhances it." Latino and African-American Muslims, he argues, face a common struggle: "The plight of blacks [in the U.S.] is similar to the plight of Latinos. We closely identify with each other in New York City."

For impoverished Latinos and African Americans living in inner cities, Islam provides material as well as spiritual support. As the government has reduced funding for urban social welfare programs over the last several decades, the urban poor have been left to fend for themselves. Muslim organizations have stepped in to provide basic services and security. Alianza Islamica, for example, has offered GED [General Educational Development] courses and HIV awareness programs, instituted clothing drives and women's groups, and initiated efforts against hunger.

Despite the growing presence of organizations such as Alianza Islamica, however, Latino Muslims are still a tiny fraction of the Latino population. Few Latinos, in fact, are even aware of their existence.

Those who convert to Islam face a certain challenge in being accepted by their surrounding communities. Galvan says that he sometimes feels alienated from the mainstream Latino population, which views Catholicism as intimately tied to Hispanic culture. However, he insists, "Defining culture by religion is not very effective, because our ancestors were Christian, Muslim, Jewish or pagan. Many Hispanics think that leaving Catholicism means rejecting their identity. We should re-evaluate how we traditionally define culture. Although some people define culture as something static," he observes, "I think defining culture as a dynamic process is more accurate."

11

American Muslims Must Be Less Hypocritical in Their Views Toward the United States and Israel

M.A. Muqtedar Khan

M.A. Muqtedar Khan is an assistant professor of political science at Adrian College in Adrian, Michigan.

American Muslims are hypocritical for not acknowledging that Arabs and Muslims are treated better in Israel and the United States than in most Middle Eastern and southern Asian nations. Israeli policy toward the Palestinians is repeatedly condemned by American Muslims, but Israel treats its Arab citizens far better than Arab nations do. Moreover, Muslims who make this charge ignore the violence perpetrated by Islamic governments. Muslims who live in the United States should admit that they enjoy more freedoms in America than they would in any other nation. By failing to recognize their hypocrisy, American Muslims are contributing to the culture of hate that is destroying the moral basis of Islam.

In the name of Allah, the most Benevolent and the most Merciful, may this memo find you in the shade of Islam enjoying the mercy, the protection, and the grace of Allah. I am writing this memo to you with the explicit purpose of inviting you to lead the American Muslim community in soul searching, reflection, and reassessment.

M.A. Muqtedar Khan, "A Memo to Fellow Muslims: An Islamic Scholar Appeals to His Fellow American Muslims in the Aftermath of the Attacks on the World Trade Center and the Pentagon," *USA Today*, vol. 130, January 2002. Copyright © 2002 by Society for the Advancement of Education. Reproduced by permission.

What happened on Sept. 11 [2001] in New York and Washington, D.C., will forever remain a horrible scar on the history of Islam and humanity. No matter how much we condemn [the terrorist attacks], and point to the Quran [Koran] and the Sunnah[1] to argue that Islam forbids the killing of innocent people, the fact remains that the perpetrators of this crime against humanity have indicated that their actions are sanctioned by Islamic values. The fact that even now several Muslim scholars and thousands of Muslims defend the accused is indicative that not all Muslims believe that the attacks are un-Islamic. This is truly sad.

> **❝ Muslims, including American Muslims, have been practicing hypocrisy on a grand scale. ❞**

Even if it were true that Israel and the U.S. are enemies of the Muslim world, I wonder what is preventing them from unleashing their nuclear arsenal against Muslims. A response that mercilessly murders thousands of innocent people, including hundreds of Muslims, is absolutely indefensible. If anywhere in your hearts there is any sympathy or understanding with those who committed this act, I invite you to ask yourself this question: Would Muhammad sanction such an act? While encouraging Muslims to struggle against injustice (Al Quran 4:135), Allah also imposes strict rules of engagement. He says in unequivocal terms that to kill an innocent being is like killing entire humanity (Al Quran 5:32). He also encourages Muslims to forgive Jews and Christians if they have committed injustices against us (Al Quran 2:109, 3:159, 5:85).

Discrimination by Muslims Is Ignored

Muslims, including American Muslims, have been practicing hypocrisy on a grand scale. They protest against the discriminatory practices of Israel, but are silent against the discriminatory practices in Muslim states. In the Persian Gulf, one can see how laws and even salaries are based on ethnic origin. This is racism, but we never hear of Muslims protesting against

1. The Sunnah is the sayings and practices of the prophet Muhammad.

such actions at international forums.

The Israeli occupation of Palestine is perhaps central to Muslim grievance against the West. While acknowledging that, I must remind you that Israel treats its 1,000,000 Arab citizens with greater respect and dignity than most Arab nations treat their citizens. Today, Palestinian refugees can settle and become citizens of the U.S., but, in spite of all the tall rhetoric of the Arab world and Quranic injunctions (24:22), no Muslim country except Jordan extends this support to them. While we loudly and consistently condemn Israel for its ill treatment of Palestinians, we are silent when Muslim regimes abuse the rights of Muslims and slaughter thousands of them. Remember [former Iraqi president] Saddam [Hussein] and his use of chemical weapons against Muslims (Kurds)? Remember the Pakistani army's excesses against Muslims (Bengalis)? Remember the Mujahideen of Afghanistan and their mutual slaughter? Have we ever condemned them for their excesses? Have we demanded international intervention or retribution against them? Do you know how the Saudis treat their minority Shiites? Have we protested the violation of their rights? Yet, we all are eager to condemn Israel—not because we care for rights and lives of the Palestinians; we don't. We condemn Israel because we hate "them."

Facing Our Hypocrisy

Muslims love to live in the U.S., but also love to hate it. Many openly claim that the U.S. is a terrorist state, but they continue to live in it. Their decision to live here is testimony that they would rather live here than anywhere else. As an Indian Muslim, I know for sure that nowhere on Earth, including India, will I get the same sense of dignity and respect that I have received in the U.S. No Muslim country will treat me as well as the U.S. has. If what happened on Sept. 11 had happened in India, the world's largest democracy, thousands of Muslims would have been slaughtered in riots on mere suspicion and there would be another slaughter after confirmation. But in the U.S., bigotry and xenophobia have been kept in check by media and leaders. In many places, hundreds of Americans have gathered around Islamic centers in symbolic gestures of protection and embrace of American Muslims. In many cities, Christian congregations have started wearing hijab to identify with fellow Muslim women. In patience and in tolerance, ordinary Americans have demonstrated their extraordinary virtues.

It is time that we acknowledge that the freedoms we enjoy in the U.S. are more desirable to us than superficial solidarity with the Muslim world. If you disagree, then prove it by packing your bags and going to whichever Muslim country you identify with. If you do not leave and do not acknowledge that you would rather live here than anywhere else, know that you are being hypocritical. It is time that we faced these hypocritical practices and struggled to transcend them. It is time that American Muslim leaders fought to purify their own lot.

For more than a decade, we have watched as Muslims in the name of Islam have committed violence against other Muslims and other peoples. We have always found a way to reconcile the vast distance between Islamic values and Muslim practices by pointing to the injustices committed upon Muslims by others. The point, however, is this—our belief in Islam and commitment to Islamic values is not contingent on the moral conduct of the U.S. or Israel. And, as Muslims, can we condone such inhuman and senseless waste of life in the name of Islam?

Hatred Is Destroying Islam

The biggest victims of hate-filled politics as embodied in the actions of several Muslim militias all over the world are Muslims themselves. Hate is the extreme form of intolerance, and when individuals and groups succumb to it, they can do nothing constructive. Militias like the Taliban [former ruling regime in Afghanistan] have allowed their hate for the West to override their obligation to pursue the welfare of their people, and as a result of their actions, not only have thousands of innocent people died in America, but thousands of people will die in the Muslim world.

The war has just begun. It will only get worse. [The terrorist groups] Hamas and Islamic Jihad may kill a few Jews, women and children included, with their suicide bombs and temporarily satisfy their lust for Jewish blood, but thousands of Palestinians ultimately will pay the price for their actions when Israel retaliates.

The culture of hate and killing is tearing away at the moral fabric of Muslim society. We are more focused on "the other" and have completely forgotten our duty to Allah. In pursuit of the inferior jihad [holy war], we have sacrificed the superior jihad. Islamic resurgence, the cherished ideals of which pursued the ultimate goal of a universally just and moral society, has been hijacked by hate and calls for murder and mayhem. If [terrorist leader] Osama bin Laden were an individual, then we would have no problem. But bin Laden has become a phenomenon—a cancer eating away at the morality of our youth and undermining the spiritual health of our future.

Today, the century-old Islamic revival is in jeopardy because we have allowed insanity to prevail over our better judgment. Yes, the U.S. played a hand in the creation of bin Laden and the Taliban, but it is we who allowed them to grow and gain such a foothold. It is our duty to police our world. It is our responsibility to prevent people from abusing Islam. It is our job to ensure that Islam is not misrepresented. We should have made sure that what happened on Sept. 11 should never have happened.

Presenting a Positive Message of Islam

It is time the leaders of the American Muslim community woke up and realized that there is more to life than competing with the American Jewish lobby for power over U.S. foreign policy. Islam is not about defeating Jews or conquering Jerusalem. It is about mercy, virtue, sacrifice, and duty. Above all, it is the pursuit of moral perfection. Nothing can be further away from moral perfection than the wanton slaughter of thousands of unsuspecting innocent people.

I hope that we will now rededicate our lives and our institutions to the search for harmony, peace, and tolerance. Let us be prepared to suffer injustice rather than commit injustices. After all, it is we who carry the divine burden of Islam and not others. We have to be morally better, more forgiving, more sacrificing than others if we wish to convince the world about the truth of our message. We cannot even be equal to others in virtue; we must excel.

It is time for soul searching. How can the message of Muhammad, who was sent as mercy to mankind, become a source of horror and fear? How can Islam inspire thousands of youths to dedicate their lives to killing others? We are supposed to invite people to Islam, not murder them.

The worst exhibition of Islam happened on our turf. We must take responsibility to undo the evil it has manifested. This is our mandate, our burden, and also our opportunity.

12

Growing Numbers Are Helping American Muslims Forge a Unified Community

Gustav Niebuhr

Gustav Niebuhr is an associate professor of religion and the media at Syracuse University in Syracuse, New York, and a leading writer on American religion.

The efforts of American Muslims to form a national community have been stymied by the increased attention paid to these Muslims since the terrorist attacks of September 11, 2001, and by the diversity of the community. The various populations, such as African Americans and South Asian and Arab immigrants, who practice Islam in the United States have differing experiences, which makes creating a united community an unprecedented task. The Islamic identity of American Muslims will likely be formed by the next generation and through the exchange of ideas over the Internet.

In Islam, midday Friday marks the time ordained for communal prayers, the Salat Al-Jumah, whose attendance is binding on Muslim men worldwide. In the United States, hundreds of mosques and prayer halls exist where Muslims can meet the obligation, from Chicago to Corpus Christi; Phoenix to Fairbanks; Brooklyn to Boston.

But one of the most intriguing sites, in terms of its proxim-

Gustav Niebuhr, "Muslims in America: Identity Develops as a Community Grows," *Carnegie Reporter*, vol. 1, Spring 2002. Copyright © 2002 by Carnegie Corporation of New York. Reproduced by permission.

ity to civic power, lies within the basement of the United States Capitol building, where a room has been reserved for an hour for this very purpose.

A Mosque Inside the Capitol

To get there one February day, a visitor descended a flight of steps from the busy first floor, passed two statues of early American settlers and rounded a corner toward a warren of committee rooms. The only indication that a sacred threshold stood nearby was a row of empty shoes pushed up against the baseboard near a frosted glass door.

On that Friday, 55 people had come to pray. Arranging themselves in six rows, they knelt on cream-colored mats spread across the wall-to-wall carpet, facing east, the direction of Mecca, Islam's holy city.

The numbers were not remarkable: many mosques, including several within a few miles of the Capitol, draw far larger crowds. But the men and women in this room, by virtue of their youth, ethnic diversity and the generous number of professionals in their ranks, were broadly representative of the larger American Muslim population. Only their closeness to national power made them more anomalous than representative.

These days, American Muslims can look back on two decades of vitally important achievements, in which they elevated the public profile of their faith by building new houses of worship, formed advocacy and educational organizations and, most recently, became increasingly involved in national political activity.

Forming a United Community

In terms of the breadth of their ethnic diversity (and the widespread suspicion with which they have often been viewed), they may most closely resemble the Roman Catholics of a century ago, who entered public consciousness as their numbers rapidly increased through immigration. But the comparison is a limited one. Nineteenth-century Catholics had the advantage of a religious hierarchy to bind them and speak for them; in that hierarchy, too, a single ethnic group—the Irish—played the dominant role. By contrast, Islam is decentralized. And so far, no national grassroots organization has emerged that would unite Muslims' disparate communities.

"It's a very Protestant system," says Zaid H. Bukhari, a fellow at Georgetown University's Center for Muslim-Christian Understanding. "There should be a collective leadership among the Muslim community," he adds, pointing out that the current "struggle" among American Muslims is for that to develop.

Mr. Bukhari is well-placed to make such observations. At Georgetown, he is director of a research project called Muslims in the American Public Square, or MAPS, in its inevitable shorthand. Previously, he served as secretary general of the Islamic Circle of North America, a Queens, N.Y.–based membership association in the mainstream of American Muslim life.

> *American Muslims can look back on two decades of vitally important achievements.*

His comments raise the question of how close Muslims are to being able to form a national community, such that people can speak of a distinctly American Muslim identity, with an attendant public voice and way of voting. And, were such a community to take shape, could it become a bridge of understanding between the U.S. and Muslim majority nations? The latter question is largely dependent on a positive resolution to the first.

Uncomfortable Attention

In the view of many Muslims, the movement toward an American Muslim identity has come under intense but conflicting pressure since the terrorist attacks of September 11th, 2001. The assaults on the World Trade Center and the Pentagon were, after all, carried out by violent extremists who claimed to act in the name of Islam, but whose deeds have been roundly condemned by many Muslim organizations and leaders here in the U.S. Nevertheless, a predictable by-product of the tragedy has been a rapid escalation of public curiosity about Islam in general and American Muslims in particular. Sales of the Qur'an, Islam's holy book, shot up in the attacks' wake, as did books by such academic writers on Islam as Karen Armstrong, John L. Esposito and Bernard Lewis.

To respond creatively to the public curiosity, the Council on American-Islamic Relations (CAIR), a Washington, D.C.–

based advocacy organization, began urging mosques nationwide to host open houses, advertising that on a specific day non-Muslim neighbors could drop by, ask questions and pick up basic material on Islam. Many mosques did so, and many of their leaders reported larger-than-expected crowds.

> **❝** *In the view of many Muslims, the movement toward an American Muslim identity has come under intense but conflicting pressure since the terrorist attacks of September 11th, 2001.* **❞**

But a part of the attention paid to American Muslims has been unnerving. In the wake of September 11th, vandals struck several mosques, and some Muslims received threatening phone calls. Perhaps even more disconcerting for some was the federal government's increased scrutiny of illegal immigrants, its detention of people who had violated their visa restrictions and its closure of Islamic charities that officials said were linked to terrorist groups.

This happened while President [George W.] Bush and others emphatically declared the U.S. not to be at war with Islam itself. That the situation might seem paradoxical to Muslims was noted by Yvonne Y. Haddad, a Georgetown [University] historian who is an authority on Islam in the U.S. For American Muslims, she says, the present is both the best and worst of times. "They have freedom," she notes, "but they're being watched."

The Demographics of American Muslims

That particular sense of living with contradiction is not unique in American Muslim life. More basic is the problem that Islam is often described as the nation's fastest-growing faith, but that its numbers remain unknown. Because the U.S. census asks no question about religious affiliation, there is no official way of quantifying the Muslim population. Without such a figure, educated guesses abound, but these range so widely—from two million at the lowest to ten million at the highest—that the estimates themselves tend to be controversial. As of 2001, Islamic organizations like CAIR began to say the Muslim population had exceeded six million.

Another contradiction is the public perception that Islam is a "new religion" in the U.S., because of its rapid growth through three decades of immigration from Asia and Africa. But the faith's roots on this side of the Atlantic go back centuries, as African American converts will point out.

Muslims set foot in North America along with Spanish explorers and English settlers, who often came with their African slaves. How many slaves were Muslim is unknown, but a handful left behind evidence of their passing, including a scholar named Omar ibn Sayyid, a West African enslaved in North Carolina, who wrote an autobiographical letter in 1831.

Organized Islamic communities began forming in the American Midwest a century ago. But Muslim religious life became publicly visible only recently, as the number of mosques increased. Nor did the rise in Islamic population derive solely from the immigrants, but also from a large influx of African American converts, especially after 1975, when Imam W. Deen Muhammad led members of the black nationalist sect, the Nation of Islam, into the orthodox fold.

These days, blacks comprise upwards of one-quarter of American Muslims, while South Asian and Arab immigrants also constitute large groups. But the ethnic mosaic reaches much further, to embrace dozens of different groups. Even cities with relatively small Muslim populations can include a highly diverse range of people with no previous experience of each other. Take Seattle, for example, where prominent members of the Muslim community include white and black converts, Arab and South Asian immigrants and groups of Somalis from East Africa and Chams from Cambodia. Latino Muslims are also a growing community: the Washington, D.C.–based American Muslim Council estimates that there are 25,000 Muslims of Hispanic heritage in U.S. metropolitan areas.

Given that that degree of diversity is not unusual, what specific factors can form a common denominator in forging a true Muslim community in America?

An Educated Community

"That's the question," says Sheik Anwar al-Awlaki, who is the imam, or spiritual leader, at Dar Al-Hijra, a major mosque in Falls Church, Virginia, a Washington suburb. "How much uniqueness American Muslims have among themselves," he says, "will determine whether they have an identity."

Elora Chowdhury, a program associate at the Ford Foundation and a Ph.D. candidate in the Women's Studies program at Clark University in Worcester, Massachusetts, agrees that identity is an increasingly important issue, but is concerned about how public perception may affect individuals as well as the Muslim community as a whole. "I think that post-September 11th," she says, "my religious background as a Muslim woman has compelled heightened public curiosity and I feel that people often expect Muslims to have external markers when, in fact, there isn't a categorical identity that all Muslims—men and women—share."

Still, among the estimated one billion Muslims globally, those in the U.S. do possess a distinctive and potentially valuable economic identity, at least when one speaks generally. American Muslims include an unusually large proportion of highly educated professionals, especially physicians and engineers, who have arrived in this nation since the sweeping reform of federal immigration laws in 1965.

Their presence helps distinguish American Muslims as "the best educated elite in the Muslim world," writes Haddad, in an essay in the book, *Muslims on the Americanization Path?* And this professional cadre sharply distinguishes American Muslims from their counterparts in immigrant communities in Europe, says Sheik al-Awlaki. "In Europe, they're the working class," he explains. "In America, they're professionals and intellectuals."

> *Muslim religious life became publicly visible only recently, as the number of mosques increased.*

A growing body of statistics lends weight to their observations. In December 2001, Bukhari's MAPS project published a demographic survey of nearly 2,000 American Muslims. Conducted by Zogby International, it reported that 58 percent of American Muslims were college graduates; three-quarters under 50, and two-thirds with an annual household income of $35,000 or more (nearly one-third said it was at least $75,000). Strikingly, the survey also found a high commitment among Muslims to civic participation: 79 percent said they were registered to vote. Of that group, the overwhelming majority said they were "highly likely" to do so. That finding in itself points to a sea-change in the basic political attitudes of American Muslims, one that suggests a Muslim political identity may be emerging. Only a decade ago, the question of whether Muslims should partici-pate in any level of politics appeared to be up for grabs.

Developments in the 1990s

Ingrid Mattson, vice president of the Plainfield, Indiana–based Islamic Society of North America, said that as late as 1989, she heard people in mosques debating whether Islamic law permit-ted Muslims to vote in a society where they were a minority. But attitudes have shifted to the point that by February 2002, CAIR was busily promoting a nationwide voter registration drive. It would take place at mosques, coinciding with Eid al-Adha, the feast that marks the culmination of the hajj, the an-nual pilgrimage to Mecca.

A rising interest in politics was not alone as an important development in Muslim life in the 1990s. During that decade, Islam became more visible on the American religious landscape, as building campaigns increased the number of mosques. In 2000, "The Mosque Study Project," a survey sponsored by four major Islamic organizations, counted 1,209 Islamic houses of worship, up from 962 in 1994, an increase of 25 percent.

As Muslims became more visible, so too did some local leaders embark on efforts at interreligious dialogue, entering into discussions with Protestant, Catholic and Jewish counter-parts. And, in a development that would seem likely to add to the growth of an American Muslim identity, the mosque-building trend relied on money raised locally, rather than from governments or organizations overseas, which had contributed to some previous work. "They decided, 'We can do it,'" Haddad says, referring to American Muslims.

At the same time, greater opportunity began to open for women within Islamic organizations, a change reflected in the experience of Mattson, who is also a professor of Islamic stud-ies at Hartford Seminary in Connecticut.

The Islamic Society, a membership organization dedicated to helping establish Muslim community centers and schools, elected her its vice president in the summer of 2001. The move, she said, starkly contrasted with the situation that prevailed in the organization in the mid-1980s. "I remember 15 years ago, being at a meeting when women weren't allowed to speak on stage," she says. Instead, they wrote their questions or comments on sheets of paper, then passed them forward for men to read aloud. But some of this momentum toward change has also produced drawbacks. The rising interest in political activism, for example, has highlighted an important, long-existing division between immigrant and native-born Muslims.

Conflicts Among Muslims

In 2000, four Muslim organizations joined forces to found the American Muslim Political Coordination Council, to rally an Islamic vote behind one of the presidential candidates. Shortly before Election Day, it endorsed George W. Bush, who had met with American Muslim representatives early in the campaign and had also spoken out against so-called "secret evidence" provisions of recent immigration laws that allow for the detention of non-citizens without full disclosure of the evidence against them. When Mr. Bush won the election as narrowly as he did, Muslims who voted for him could claim a vital role in his victory. But the committee's decision also exacerbated an old rift. Many African American Muslims felt they had not been consulted about the endorsement, a lack of recognition that rankled, given the high proportion of blacks within the overall Muslim population.

> *[Fifty-eight] percent of American Muslims were college graduates; three-quarters under 50, and two-thirds with an annual income of $35,000 or more.*

Partisan politics, Mattson says, can reinforce class and ethnic distinctions. "Some of the African Americans would see the immigrants as falling into supporting an economic order that is inherently oppressive to African Americans, so that can exacerbate conflicts," she says, adding that politics "forces you into categories that you don't have to have in a religious community."

Aamir A. Rehman, director of outreach at the Islamic Society of Boston, also ponders some of the conflicts that can be created by different cultural and ethnic groups' experiences and expectations about the practice of Islam in the U.S. "In

America," he says, "Muslims often worship side by side with people from all over the Muslim world. Exposure to this rich diversity of cultures can be stimulating but also confusing for some. But this uniquely American situation also presents an opportunity to focus on the study and practice of Islam—on what Islam is all about—rather than on the cultural features that attend Islam in any particular country or region."

Islam carries an ideal of a universal community. Belonging to the ummah, the community of the faith, should trump race, class and ethnicity. That vision of equality becomes visible during the pilgrimage to Mecca, itself one of Islam's Five Pillars of religious practice. Muslims are required, if they are able, to make the journey once in their lifetimes. In Mecca, the hundreds of thousands of pilgrims follow the same rituals, and the men among them dress alike, each wearing a simple garment of two large pieces of unstitched and seamless cloth.

An Influential Mosque

The ideal of unity has never been far from American Muslim consciousness, perhaps a recognition of the unprecedented task of bringing together such a wide-ranging group. In annual meetings, Mattson says, Muslim organizations have prominently displayed a passage from the Qur'an as a theme for discussion: "O surely we have created you of a male and a female, and made you tribes and families that you may know each other." The emphasis on unity is also often reflected at the local level, which is really the scene of much action in American Islamic life.

The All-Dulles Area Muslim Society in Herndon, Virginia, familiarly known by its acronym, ADAMS, offers one example. The mosque is among the most prominent on the East Coast and its constituency is decidedly multi-ethnic, with immigrants from Asia and Africa, as well as African American, Latino and white converts.

In an interview, Imam Mohamed Magid, the tall, broad-shouldered and bearded spiritual leader, emphasized the symbolic value of the mosque's having had four different speakers at [2001's] Eid al-Fitr, the holiday that concludes the dawn-to-dusk fast at the end of the lunar month of Ramadan. Two speakers, he said, were African American, the third a Yemeni immigrant and the fourth himself, a native of Sudan. "That shows the acceptance of the community," Imam Magid said, referring to the mosque. "We don't have an ethnic community dominating."

90

The mosque stands out in another way, too, as one of those Muslim institutions that will alter its local religious landscape. [In fall 2001] the mosque broke ground for a new building, a $4.5 million project to house a congregation now so large that it must worship in shifts.

Keeping the Next Generation Involved

Imam Magid looks to the next generation of American Muslims to shape an Islamic identity in this country. "The children of American Muslims play together without recognizing ethnic backgrounds," he notes. "When our children ask each other, 'Where do you come from?' They answer, 'I come from America,' or 'I come from Virginia.'" The implicit message, he says, which he shares with parents at the mosque, is: "America has the ability to create a collective identity, even though you come from different cultural backgrounds."

By raising the issue of children, he touched on a central issue of concern among American Muslims. How the next generation will carry on the faith is a question that has always concerned religious minorities in the U.S. But its urgency among Muslims can be glimpsed on an Internet site that specializes in selling audiotapes of prominent Islamic scholars. The number one lecture listed there focuses on retaining the loyalty of Muslim children to their faith.

> **"** *The ideal of unity has never been far from American Muslim consciousness.* **"**

In the view of Sheik al-Awlaki, at Dar Al-Hijra, a key to keeping younger Muslims active as Muslims lies in the use of English as the predominant language within Islamic organizations. "Whenever there's a switch in language from ethnic to English, you would suddenly find more participation among the young," he said. "It's immediate. English is their mother tongue."

This group will shape the future of Muslims in the United States, Sheik al-Awlaki says. Already a religious leader at the age of 30, he was born in New Mexico but raised mostly in his parents' native Yemen, before returning to the United States at 18. He refers to the younger generation as "Muslim baby boomers."

The sons and daughters of immigrants and converts, they have a keener interest in civil rights and politics than their parents do, he says. But how they will exert their leadership is something he cannot predict.

New Methods of Communication

Arabic is Islam's sacred language. The Prophet Muhammad received the Qur'an in Arabic from the Archangel Gabriel. Any rendering of the Islamic holy book into another tongue is considered an interpretation, not a translation. But as a means of communication, the majority of Muslims do not use Arabic, either globally or in the U.S.

Throughout the 1980s and 1990s, mosques and Islamic organizations increasingly switched to doing business in English, rather than relying on the native languages of their immigrant members. [In 2001] the change occurred at Dar Al-Hijra in Falls Church. "English is a determinate factor of the American Muslim identity," Sheik al-Awlaki says.

The use of English as the common medium of communication among American Muslim groups has broader implications, too, not least for the influence that they may have on Muslims overseas.

In an essay for the book, *Muslim Minorities in the West*, the Moroccan scholar Abdul Hamid Lotfi said that American Muslims have steadily expanded their presence on the Internet, rather than attempting to make themselves heard over the far more expensive media of radio or television. The result, he says, was the creation of a "Muslim cyberspace, where ideas are exchanged and tested" in a democratic forum, outside the traditional grounds of the university or mosque.

The Internet, of course, is international, allowing ideas and discussions begun in the U.S. to find an audience in any number of nations overseas, a medium through which the Islamic population in this country could speak to its counterparts elsewhere.

But because the Internet is still so new, its effect in this area can only be conjectured. So when American Muslims speak about the effect they can have as bridge-builders between the United States and Muslims abroad, they tend to cite the value of personal contacts—and also to raise a caution about how those contacts can be undercut by the impact of American foreign policy decisions.

American Muslims Can Play a Valuable Role

The latter issue is often raised in interviews with Muslims, usually with the expressed concern that the U.S. must be perceived by their counterparts overseas as taking a more active role in attempting to resolve certain long-term conflicts. Those conflicts are between the Israelis and Palestinians, the Pakistanis and the Indians over Kashmir, and the Russians and Chechnyans. But if it is possible to step beyond these weighty issues for a moment, then the possibility of what American Muslims might do for the image of their country in other parts of the world is a tantalizing one upon which to reflect.

The interview with Imam Magid, for example, took place the day before he was to depart on the pilgrimage to Mecca. In the conversation, he noted that before returning to the U.S. he was stopping in Sudan to speak at a university in the capital, Khartoum.

His audience, he explained, might be interested to hear about the life of his mosque in Virginia, including how other religious communities offered to help after anti-Muslim graffiti was painted on its exterior in the wake of the September 11th tragedy. "I think some of them might be shocked that some Jews and some Christians volunteered to paint our walls," he said.

A story like this reflects a situation that some academic authorities have remarked on as an important new piece of American Muslim life, post–September 11th. Many Muslims in this country, they say, were touched by gestures of kindness and concern from their non-Muslim neighbors during the tense weeks after the terror attacks. Some women wore headscarves as a way of showing support for Muslim women, while men and women alike called local mosques and offered to step in and help those—say, with grocery shopping—who felt afraid to go outside for fear of being harassed.

But regardless of how widely such information is shared, Mattson predicts that American Muslims will have "increasing influence" abroad. "Muslims in other parts of the world are going to receive American culture, and part of that includes American Muslim culture," she says.

She has her own recent example. When she was elected the Islamic Society's vice president, the event was covered by television stations in Egypt and the United Arab Emirates. Later, Egyptian television followed up by interviewing one of the society's officials, a discussion that turned on the role of American Muslim women. "And that's getting to millions of people in Egypt," she points out.

"I'm an academic," she says. "I see how ideas have come down through history. And I do believe that ideas filter down and have an impact on things that are common knowledge, things that are known by the average person."

13

Americans Misunderstand Islam

Russell Reza-'Khaliq Gonzaga

Russell Reza-'Khaliq Gonzaga is a poet, writer, and performance artist.

While most Americans who practice Islam are either African Americans or immigrants from the Middle East and South Asia, the religion—especially the mystical form of Islam known as Sufism—is appealing to an increasing number of white Americans. Despite the growing popularity of Islam, many Americans continue to view the religion as a foreign faith that promotes aggression. Many also believe that Islamic leaders encourage hatred of the United States, particularly in the wake of the September 11, 2001, terrorist attacks on the United States, which were perpetrated by Islamic hijackers. In reality Islam is a highly diverse religion that is not bound to a specific worldview. Americans should respect Islam and its followers.

It was 1989, shortly after the fall of the [Berlin] Wall, and I was just a young Filipino American drawn to the underground culture and intensity of Berlin. I had taken to hanging out with Kurdish and Turkish friends while in Germany. I found their easygoing attitude and humorous outlook refreshing and oddly familiar. They were not unlike the African American and Latino friends I had grown up with back home.

On a Friday night just a week after Germany's World Cup victory, we stopped in a falafel restaurant in the Kruzberg section of Berlin. My friends pointed out that the place had to be

Russell Reza-'Khaliq Gonzaga, "One Nation Under Allah," *ColorLines*, vol. 5, Fall 2002, pp. 27–29. Copyright © 2002 by ColorLines Magazine. Reproduced by permission.

good because of the number of Turks who were dining there at the time. As we were waiting, my eyes wandered around the restaurant. There were several family groups with many children. Some of the women dressed like the German women and others wore the conservative garb I recognized as the typical outfit of a Turkish woman: large pattern-printed scarves hooded over their clean and unpainted faces; loose-fitting blouses with long sleeves; long, pressed skirts hemmed no higher than mid-calf, and mid-heeled leather loafers on stocking-covered feet. It was a look that conveyed respectability and conventionality. This was nothing special in that part of Berlin, but my gaze was arrested by a woman accompanied by two others, each dressed in the Turkish manner. This one woman was so very "Aryan" in her features that even with her hair covered, I could see from her flaxen eyebrows and lashes that she was very blond. Her alabaster skin was so fair you could practically see the blood vessels just under the surface, and her eyes were the lightest of blue. This was not what I had come to expect of a Muslima.

Race and Islam

I hadn't realized that I was staring, gawking really. This is considered very rude in Islamic cultures. I was jarred out of my trance by the sharp elbow of one of my companions. "Hey man! What are you doing? You don't stare, especially at a woman. . . ." Still bewildered, I made the situation worse by thoughtlessly saying in a loud voice, "But she's WHITE!" The entire restaurant turned to look. Very embarrassed, my friends tried to apologize for me in Turkish as they pulled me out the front doors and into the street. "What's wrong with you, man? You crazy or something?"

> *It's evident . . . that Islam has been seen as something of a 'non-white' faith.*

It wasn't until then that I realized how race had so defined my perception of Islam. Growing up in an urban American city did nothing to prepare me for the reality of Islam in the rest of the world. An assumption I had made about Islam was that, among other things, it was not white.

African Americans and Islam

*"We have created you from one male and one female,
and then We made you into different races and tribes
so that you may (recognize and) know one another."*
(The Qur'an 49:13)

Brother Abu Qadir Al-Amin is the Imam [spiritual leader] of the San Francisco Muslim Community Center. A strong and stout African American with Southern roots, Imam Al-Amin speaks with an authority not only from his intimate study of the Qur'an and Islam, but also from a great deal of street knowledge.

> *It may be surprising to find that Islam [has] found its way into the hearts of a great number of white Americans.*

"To look at [the] racialization of Islam here in America, you have to look at the history of slavery. Islam came here on the slave ships," Imam Al-Amin says. "Even though the practice of Islam was banned amongst the slaves of the antebellum South, elements of it remained as a part of our oral tradition."

Out of these roots, early movements developed, such as the Moorish Science Temple founded by Noble Drew Ali in the 1920s. Ali's message of dignity and economic independence had strong appeal to depression-era African Americans. These teachings, along with those of black nationalist Marcus Garvey, were strong influences on the next generation of African American Muslims.

Imam Al-Amin's involvement with Islam, like many African American Muslims of his generation, started in the Nation of Islam under its charismatic founder, Elijah Muhammad. The doctrine of the Nation was well known for its racial component.

It was this "White Devil" doctrine that shocked and terrified America, despite the many other positive elements to their movement. This reverse psychology was a means to shake African Americans out of their own internalized oppression. Imam Al-Amin explains, "Whites had put themselves up on a pedestal, practically attributing themselves a divine status, and a lot of us had bought into that, consciously and subconsciously. We had to hear a wake-up call out of that nightmare."

By the time of Elijah Muhammad's death in 1975, the Nation of Islam had established over 76 temples nationwide with an estimated 100,000 members. Leadership of the Nation was ceremoniously passed on to Elijah's son, Warith Deen Mohammed, by election. Almost immediately W.D. Mohammed began to dismantle the Nation as he started to lead the members into the practice of Sunni (Orthodox) Islam.

> *Islam is a very present element of American culture and society.*

Today, African Americans comprise over 40 percent of the estimated 6 to 8 million Muslims in America today (the largest racial group). All members did not entirely accept this move towards orthodoxy, however. By the early 1980's, the then disgruntled and now controversial Louis Farrakhan reorganized the Nation of Islam and brought this contingent back to the teachings of Elijah Muhammad. The two camps held a long-standing animosity for each other, but as leaders of both factions will point out, not a drop of blood was spilled between them in the years of this separation. Disagreement was kept on the rhetorical and theological level and both still focused on the common goal of strengthening the African American community.

Muslim Immigration

Islam has been seen as a significant part of the African heritage of black Americans. But as the immigrant population grew, it became apparent that Islam belonged to another group of Americans as well. From 1878 to 1924, a wave of immigrants came from what was then called Greater Syria. These Syrian, Jordanian, and Lebanese immigrants were, for the most part, uneducated laborers. Many of these disenchanted migrants returned to their homelands, but those who did stay somehow managed to establish Islamic communities. Enclaves in places like Iowa and North Dakota developed. Muslims congregated in homes and rented halls. Later these enclaves started to develop in Detroit, Pittsburgh, and Indiana. But this growth almost came to a halt in 1924 due to the Asian Exclusion Act (Arabs were classified as Asians) and the Johnson-Reed Immigration Act, which slowed the immigration of Asians (including Arabs) to a mere trickle.

America was not to see a significant wave of Muslim immigration until 1948, when the first Palestinian refugees arrived after the creation of Israel. With the McCarran-Walter Act of 1952 and major immigration reform of 1965,[1] the population of Muslim immigrants continued growing. Muslim Americans whose ancestr[ies] trace back to Africa, the Middle East, and South Asia have formed significant communities across the country. But now, after 9/11, this social fabric is in danger of being torn apart.

Western Projections

"We should come to know our Shadow or else there is a strong tendency to project our Shadow upon others."
(Carl Jung)

It's evident from the current racial profiling that Islam has been seen as something of a "non-white" faith. Part of the reason for this is that Islam developed here in America through non-white communities. Add to this the element of the European cultural and ancestral backgrounds of white Americans. During the Crusades, Europe had practically defined itself in terms of its resistance to Islam.

As celebrated British theologian and historian Karen Armstrong explains, "The West misunderstands Islam largely because we've got a deep cultural prejudice that is as deeply ingrained as our anti-Semitism, which developed alongside it from about the time of the Crusades. We've got into the habit of projecting our own shortcomings onto Islam, just as we did upon the Jews."

In today's lexicon of the dreaded *burqa*[2] and fanatical woman-hating clerics, it may be hard to remember a time when Islam represented wanton sensuality and licentiousness. During the Victorian Age especially, Western scholars viewed Islam with a mix of fascination and revulsion.

"Today when many people in the West are trying to shed the sexual repressions of their Christian past, we say that Islam is a sexually repressed religion," Armstrong points out.

Sexual repression is just one issue the West projects upon Is-

---

1.The McCarran-Walter Act abolished racial restrictions for immigration while creating a strict quota system, which the 1965 reform eliminated.   2. This is traditional Muslim women's clothing that covers the face and sometimes the body.

lam. Class and gender also take on this distortion. Armstrong continues, "At a time in the Middle Ages when Europe was extremely hierarchical, we blamed Islam for giving too much power to menials like slaves and women. Today we've thrown that off, and we blame Islam for being oppressive to women. Again, we've reversed the old stereotype, not because we've found out anything about Islam necessarily, but because we've got into a cultural habit of making Islam the opposite of us."

These cultural projections continue today in the mainstream media, which has placed attention and emphasis upon the more extreme, yet relatively small, factions of the Islamic world. Muslims are frequently pictured as militantly aggressive and fanatical. What does this say about what Americans are projecting? Throughout the history of Western civilization, Islam has been portrayed as "exotic" at best, the "enemy menace" for the most part, but always as the "other."

Growing Appeal

While Islam was established among African Americans and the immigration of Arab and South Asian Muslims continued to grow independently, it may be surprising to find that Islam also found its way into the hearts of a great number of white Americans. During the experimental 1960s, many were searching for the meaning to life and existence outside the Western paradigm. Along with the gurus, the Human Potential Movement seminars, and the transcendental meditation, a good number of seekers started investigating Sufism—the mystical practice within Islam.

Sufi orders have existed in America since 1910, but it was the '60s that brought it into the landscape of American culture. The '70s marked the arrival of several sheikhs ("teachers") of undisputed Islamic lineage. This firmly established a number of Sufi orders' presence here in America. Loved for its universalist principles and devotional practices, Sufism's popularity and growth have been strong ever since.

> *In every religion there is Love, yet Love has no religion.*
> *Love is like an ocean, without borders and shores*
>   *where so many drown,*
> *Yet regretful cries are not to be heard.*

> (Jalaluddin Rumi)

Most dervishes ("Sufi practitioners") in America are white.

Shaikh Rashid Patch explains, "Exposure to Sufism in America was initially academic. In this relatively early stage in (Sufism's) development in this hemisphere, it has been those privileged enough to go to college or to travel to Islamic countries who have been exposed to it."

Rashid, a former U.S. Marine who converted to Islam, is of Irish descent. His frequent smile and a hearty laugh are practically the trademarks of dervishes. Far from being a fundamentalist of any sort, Rashid, like many Muslims, is involved in a number of interfaith efforts, and he remains dedicated to peace. But Shaikh Patch takes an uncharacteristically terse tone when speaking about the developments since [the September 11, 2001, terrorist attacks].

"This racial profiling is insanity. Why weren't white men profiled after the Oklahoma bombing or during the Unabomber scare? Most Americans don't even have a clear idea of what a Muslim is, and 'Arab' isn't even distinct enough. An 'Arab' could be anyone!"

Shaikh Patch continued, "When I was young, I can remember Catholicism being racialized. It became a big issue in the election of John F. Kennedy. When I was nine years old, back in the '50s, I remember members of the KKK shooting at me. To them, me and my family were not "white." We were something else, and that something else happened to be Catholic. Sounds crazy, eh? Well, racism and bigotry don't have much to do with sanity."

Islam Is Diverse

After 9/11, mainstream America found itself in a quandary over this tragedy. *Why would anyone attack us? Who are these people?*

In the struggle for answers, a great number of Americans began to settle for the easy answers that some media pundits were serving up like junk food. "Islam is a religion based on war and aggression," "Muslims stand in opposition of everything that America stands for," "The Islamic world hates America." The fact is, however, the Islamic world is hardly monolithic in its view of anything. Being just about the most racially, culturally, and ideologically diverse of religions in the world, it is virtually impossible to claim any one view as *the* Muslim worldview. Moreover, the plain fact is that Islam is a very present element of American culture and society. It is still one of the fastest growing faiths in the world and in America *even* after 9/11.

"In my short life span, I have seen Islam influence American culture in clear ways as well as subtle," says Imam Al-Amin. "No longer can America only acknowledge Judaism and Christianity as its only major faiths. Islam must also be included and recognized for its worth. America must respect its own diversity. Our nation's inclusion and future in the world community may count on it."

Organizations to Contact

The editors have compiled the following list of organizations concerned with the issues debated in this book. The descriptions are derived from materials provided by the organizations. All have publications or information available for interested readers. The list was compiled on the date of publication of the present volume; names, addresses, phone and fax numbers, and e-mail addresses may change. Be aware that many organizations take several weeks or longer to respond to inquires, so allow as much time as possible.

American Islamic Forum for Democracy
1301 E. McDowell Rd., Suite 202, Phoenix, AZ 85006
(602) 254-1840
e-mail: info@aifdemocracy.org • Web site: www.aifdemocracy.org

The forum is a collection of American Muslims who believe that the practice of Islam is compatible with the American principles of democracy. It supports the separation of church and state and complete allegiance to the United States. The Web site features opinions and commentaries.

American Muslim Council (AMC)
1005 W. Webster Ave., Suite 3, Chicago, IL 60614
(773) 248-3390
e-mail: info@amcnational.org • Web site: www.amcnational.org

The AMC is an organization that aims to increase the participation of American Muslims in politics and public policy. The AMC also seeks to encourage a larger presence for American Muslims in mainstream public life.

Arab American Institute (AAI)
1600 K St. NW, Suite 601, Washington, DC 20006
(202) 429-9210 • fax: (202) 429-9214
e-mail: aai@aaiusa.org • Web site: www.aaiusa.org

AAI is a nonprofit organization committed to the political and civic empowerment of Arab Americans. Resources available on the Web site include weekly columns by its president, reports on civil liberties after September 11, 2001, and a resource packet on Arab Americans, the Middle East, and Islam, consisting of articles, speeches, polls, charts, and other information.

Council on American-Muslim Relations (CAIR)
453 New Jersey Ave. SE, Washington, DC 20003
(202) 488-8787 • fax: (202) 488-0833
e-mail: cair@cair-net.org • Web site: www.cair-net.org

CAIR is a nonprofit organization that challenges stereotypes of Islam and Muslims and offers an Islamic perspective on public policy issues.

It also promotes a positive image of Islam and Muslims in America and aims to empower the American Muslim community. Its publications include action alerts, news briefs, and reports such as *The Mosque in America: National Portrait.*

Islamic Circle of North America (ICNA)
166-26 Eighty-ninth Ave., Jamaica, NY 11432
(718) 658-1199 • fax: (718) 658-1255
e-mail: info@icna.org • Web site: www.icna.org

ICNA's goal is to establish an Islamic system of life in the United States, one that is based on the laws of Islam and the teachings of the prophet Muhammad. All American Muslims are welcome to join if they adhere to the goals of the program, which include studying Islamic writings. The *Message* is the organization's monthly magazine.

Islamic Information Center of America (IICA)
PO Box 4052, Des Plaines, IL 60016
(847) 541-8141 • fax: (847) 824-8436
e-mail: president@iica.org • Web site: www.iica.org

IICA is a nonprofit organization that provides information about Islam to Muslims, the media, and the general public. Articles published by the center cover topics such as the Muslim diet and theology.

Islamic Society of North America (ISNA)
PO Box 38, Plainfield, IN 46168
(317) 839-8157 • fax: (317) 839-1840
Web site: www.isna.net

The ISNA is an association of Muslim individuals and organizations that offers a universal platform for supporting Muslim communities, developing strong interfaith relations, and creating educational and social programs. Papers are archived on the Web site, covering issues such as Islam in prisons, the challenges facing American Muslims, and teachings on Islam.

Islamic Supreme Council of America (ISCA)
17195 Silver Pkwy. #401, Fenton, MI 48430
(810) 593-1222 • fax: (810) 815-0518
e-mail: staff@islamicsupremecouncil.org
Web site: www.islamicsupremecouncil.org

The ISCA is a nonprofit religious organization that seeks to find solutions based on traditional Islamic scholarship to contemporary issues facing American Muslims. The organization also aims to educate government officials on Muslim culture and history through publications, meetings, and conferences. Books on Islamic beliefs and practices are available for purchase from the Web site.

Karamah: Muslim Women Lawyers for Human Rights
1420 Sixteenth St. NW, Washington, DC 20036
(202) 234-7302 • fax: (202) 234-7304
e-mail: karamah@karamah.org • Web site: www.karamah.org

Karamah is an organization that supports the human rights of Muslims in the United States and throughout the world and aims to improve the treatment of women in Islamic communities. It seeks to achieve these goals through activism, advocacy, and education. Speeches and articles are archived on the Web site, covering issues such as women's rights, religious freedom, and Islam and the West.

Muslim American Society (MAS)
PO Box 1896, Falls Church, VA 22041
(703) 998-6525 • fax: (703) 998-6526
e-mail: mas@masnet.org • Web site: www.masnet.org

The society is a not-for-profit organization that performs charitable, religious, cultural, and educational activities that uplift American Muslims. MAS publishes the quarterly magazine *American Muslim*; articles from the magazine and from outside publications can be found on the Web site.

Muslim Public Affairs Council (MPAC)
110 Maryland Ave. NE, Suite 304, Washington, DC 20002
(202) 547-7701 • fax: (202) 547-7704
Web site: www.mpac.org

MPAC is a public service agency that works to improve the civil rights of American Muslims, promote a strong American Muslim community, and provide accurate and reliable information to the U.S. government and media. Information on hate crimes and antiterrorism campaigns is available on the Web site, along with commentaries and position papers such as *Counterproductive Counterterrorism: How Anti-Islamic Rhetoric Is Impeding America's Homeland Security*.

Web Sites

Center for Islamic Pluralism (CIP), www.islamicpluralism.org

CIP is a think tank that assists moderate American Muslims in their efforts toward becoming a respected element of the American interfaith community and educates the American public about moderate Islam and the threat posed to Americans by radical Islam. Articles dealing with Islamic issues in both the United States and abroad are available on the Web site.

Daniel Pipes Homepage, www.danielpipes.org

This Web site contains numerous articles, interviews, and speeches about Islam and American Muslims that were written by Daniel Pipes, the director of the Middle East Forum and a prize-winning columnist for the *New York Sun* and *Jerusalem Post*.

Bibliography

Books

Zahid H. Bukhari, ed. *Muslims' Place in the American Public Square: Hope, Fears, and Aspirations.* Walnut Creek, CA: AltaMira Press, 2004.

Jocelyne Cesari *When Islam and Democracy Meet: Muslims in Europe and the United States.* New York: Palgrave Macmillan, 2004.

Edward E. Curtis IV *Islam in Black America: Identity, Liberation, and Difference in African-American Islamic Thought.* Albany: State University of New York Press, 2002.

Robert Dannin *Black Pilgrimage to Islam.* New York: Oxford University Press, 2002.

Tom Diaz and Barbara Newman *Lightning out of Lebanon: Hezbollah Terrorists on American Soil.* New York: Presidio Press, 2005.

Steven Emerson *American Jihad: The Terrorists Living Among Us.* New York: Free Press, 2002.

Ron Geaves, ed. *Islam and the West Post 9/11.* Aldershot, UK: Ashgate, 2004.

Yvonne Yasbeck Haddad *Not Quite American?: The Shaping of Arab and Muslim Identity in the United States.* Waco, TX: Baylor University Press, 2004.

Yvonne Yasbeck Haddad, ed. *Muslims in the West: From Sojourners to Citizens.* New York: Oxford University Press, 2002.

Asama Gul Hasan *American Muslims: The New Generation.* New York: Continuum, 2001.

David Horowitz *Unholy Alliance: Radical Islam and the American Left.* Washington, DC: Regnery, 2004.

Harvey Kushner *Holy War on the Home Front: The Secret Islamic Terror Network in the United States.* New York: Sentinel, 2004.

Bruce B. Lawrence *New Faiths, Old Fears: Muslims and Other Asian Immigrants in American Religious Life.* New York: Columbia University Press, 2002.

Michael S. Lee *Healing the Nation: The Arab American Experience After September 11.* Washington, DC: Arab American Institute, 2002.

Karen Isaksen Leonard   *Muslims in the United States: The State of Research.* New York: Russell Sage Foundation, 2003.

Iftikhar H. Malik   *Islam and Modernity: Muslims in Europe and the United States.* London: Pluto Press, 2004.

Aminah Mohammad-Arif, trans. by Sarah Patey   *Salaam America: South Asian Muslims in New York.* London: Anthem Press, 2002.

Daniel Pipes   *Militant Islam Reaches America.* New York: W.W. Norton, 2002.

Carolyn Moxley Rouse   *Engaged Surrender: African American Women and Islam.* Berkeley: University of California Press, 2004.

Stephen Schwartz   *The Two Faces of Islam: Saudi Fundamentalism and Its Role in Terror.* New York: Anchor, 2003.

Robert Spencer   *Onward Muslim Soldiers: How Jihad Still Threatens America and the West.* Washington, DC: Regnery, 2003.

Vibert L. White   *Inside the Nation of Islam: A Historical and Personal Testimony by a Black Muslim.* Gainesville: University Press of Florida, 2001.

Michael Wolfe, ed.   *Taking Back Islam: America Muslims Reclaim Their Faith.* New York: Rodale, 2002.

Richard Wormser   *American Islam: Growing Up Muslim in America.* New York: Walker, 2002.

Periodicals

Riad Z. Abdelkarim   "American Muslims and 9/11," *Washington Report on Middle East Affairs*, September/October 2002.

Hisham Aidi   "Urban Islam and the War on Terror," *ColorLines*, Winter 2002–2003.

Christine Armario   "US Latinas Seek Answers in Islam," *Christian Science Monitor*, December 27, 2004.

Bill Berkowitz   "African American Muslims: A Clear and Present Danger?" *Z Magazine*, June 2003.

Sarah Downey and Michael Hirsh   "A Safe Haven?" *Newsweek*, September 30, 2002.

Jim Edwards   "Statistics Don't Bear Out Feared Wave of Bias Cases Against Muslims," *New Jersey Law Journal*, June 10, 2002.

Steven Emerson, interviewed by Verena Kolb   "Emerson Has Eye on Militant Islam," *Insight on the News*, January 28, 2002.

Hillel Fradkin   "America in Islam," *Public Interest*, Spring 2004.

Laurie Goodstein   "Stereotyping Rankles Silent, Secular Majority of American Muslims," *New York Times*, December 23, 2001.

Muqtedar Khan   "Putting the American in 'American Muslim,'" *New York Times*, September 7, 2003.

Jane Lampman   "Muslim in America," *Christian Science Monitor*, January 10, 2002.

Gerald A. Larue   "Islam in the United States," *Humanist*, March/April 2002.

John Leo   "Pushing the Bias Button," *U.S. News & World Report*, June 9, 2003.

Salim Muwakkil   "The Forgotten History of Islam in America," *In These Times*, September 16, 2002.

Ahmed Nassef   "Listen to Muslim Silent Majority in US," *Christian Science Monitor*, April 21, 2004.

Asra Q. Nomani   "Shaking Up Islam in America," *Time*, September 13, 2004.

Daniel Pipes   "The Danger Within: Militant Islam in America," *Commentary*, November 2001.

Daniel Pipes and Khalid Duran   "Faces of American Islam," *Policy Review*, August/September 2002.

Stephen Schwartz   "Reading, Writing, and Extremism," *Weekly Standard*, June 2, 2003.

Shibley Telhami   "Arab and Muslim America: A Snapshot," *Brookings Review*, Winter 2002.

Time   "As American as . . . Although Scapegoated, Muslims, Sikhs, and Arabs Are Patriotic, Integrated— and Growing," October 1, 2001.

Index